MASTERING DATA TO WIN

SAIL
TO WIN

With thanks to:

Our sponsors

The Stella Maris *team for their input and photos*

ClubSwan Racing / Studio Borlenghi for their photos

MASTERING DATA TO WIN

Understand your instruments to
Make the Right Calls & Win Races

Mark Chisnell & Gilberto Pastorella

FERNHURST
BOOKS

Published in 2023 by Fernhurst Books Limited

The Windmill, Mill Lane, Harbury, Leamington Spa, Warwickshire. CV33 9HP, UK

Tel: +44 (0) 1926 337488 | www.fernhurstbooks.com

A catalogue record for this book is available from the British Library

ISBN 978-1912621668

Front cover photograph © Antonio Otero

Designed by Daniel Stephen

Printed in the UK by Halstan

THE AUTHORS

PROFESSIONAL NAVIGATORS

Mark Chisnell

Mark Chisnell's writing includes 18 books, with translations in six languages. He has written narrative non-fiction books about adventure and endeavour at sea, as well as suspense and mystery thrillers. Mark has also written technical books on the art and science of racing sailboats. His journalism on travel, sport and technology has been published in some of the world's leading magazines and newspapers, including *Esquire* (UK), the *Sunday Telegraph*, *Daily Telegraph*, *Guardian*, *New Zealand Herald* and *South China Morning Post* as well as many sailing magazines internationally.

Mark Chisnell

Mark began his writing with travel stories, while hitch-hiking around the world. He got a job sweeping up and making tea with the British America's Cup team in Australia in 1987 to earn the money to get home. He worked his way onto the boat as navigator and has sailed and worked with six more America's Cup teams since then. He's also won three World Championships, sailing as navigator.

Mark Chisnell is now Rules Advisor at Ineos Britannia, the America's Cup team of four-time Olympic gold medallist Sir Ben Ainslie.

Gilberto Pastorella

Gilberto was born in Milan, Italy. He started sailing when he was 10 and the sport quickly became a big part of his life. He became a dinghy instructor in 2005 and skippered his first racer-cruiser offshore in 2007.

In the meantime, he quickly realised that his mind enjoyed dealing with numbers and mathematical problems; he graduated in applied mathematics in 2011.

From there, he always tried to keep these two passions together, working as a navigator for various teams but also opening an online-offline school to teach the secrets of numbers on board to

Gilberto Pastorella

other sailors and working for companies that were installing and developing electronic systems.

Currently he races both inshore and offshore and works as a data and technology consultant for companies in different industries. Gilberto translated the previous version of this book, *Sail Smart*, into Italian. When we were looking for someone to update it with Mark, Gilberto was the obvious choice.

CONTENTS

FOREWORD 9

INTRODUCTION 11

CHAPTER 1 The Role of the Navigator 13

CHAPTER 2 The Key Elements of Data On Board 17

CHAPTER 3 Setting Up an Instrument System 35

CHAPTER 4 Some Instrument Techniques 61

CHAPTER 5 Instrument Techniques Using the Polar Tables 69

CHAPTER 6 Data Collection & Performance Analysis 83

CHAPTER 7 What's Next 91

CREDITS 92

Ian Walker

FOREWORD

Everywhere you look in society there is a rise in the importance of data and a need to not only create good, clean data but also to understand its value. As the saying goes, beware 'rubbish in, rubbish out …' Whether you like it or not, the rising importance of data is a fact of life, and it is increasingly a fact of life in performance sailing. Mastering data will improve your team's performance, particularly your starts, and lies at the heart of your strategy and tactics. As a racing professional helmsman and tactician I have become increasingly dependent on that data and those who help to manage it.

Fortunately I am lucky enough to have sailed with many of the best navigators in the world, including Mark Chisnell, with whom we won the Gold Roman Bowl last year (1st overall IRC Round the Island Race 2022). The best navigators stand out by knowing what information to share and when. As an example, in a quiet period they may discuss the geometry of the next leg or some thoughts on strategy or the wind or current, but as you approach an important layline they will not only be giving their best estimate of the calculated time to the layline but they may also share some 'What Ifs' such as 'we are one minute to layline but we would lay if the wind shifts 10 degrees to the right …'

For this information to be valuable it also has to be as accurate as possible (within the limitations of your electronics package and the conditions). This is the reason why this book is fundamental reading not only for any aspiring navigator but I would suggest for all members of the crew. I think it will open peoples' eyes to the importance of the role and the need to dedicate time to calibrating your instruments and refining your polars.

As the book says, 'navigator' is not really the right term now for somebody whose role has expanded well beyond trying to work out where you are and which direction to head in. It is one of the most interesting roles on board and I think if I had my time again in sailing, I would maybe come back as a navigator. Good navigators need to be very well prepared, well organised and good under pressure – I would suggest that reading this book is a pretty good place to start that preparation!

Ian Walker
General Manager, North Sails UK
Olympic Silver Medallist, 1996 & 2000
Skipper of Volvo Ocean Race winner *Abu Dhabi Ocean Racing* (2014/15)

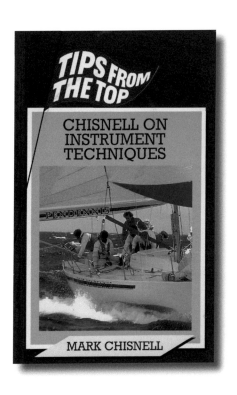

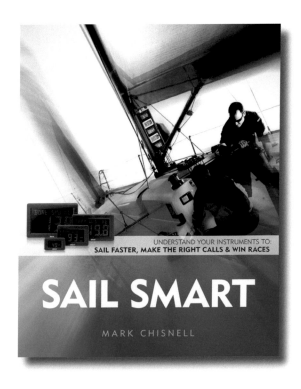

Introduction

A change in the *Racing Rules of Sailing* in the mid-1980s led to performance-related electronics being allowed on sailing boats for racing. Since then, advances in modern technology and a different type of racing have all helped to alter the navigator's job to the point where it is almost a misnomer and has got little to do with the original job description of 'bringing the boat safely from point A to point B'. Today, the problem is how best to process the myriad of data that comes out of the instrument system, understand the story that it is telling and make it useful for the team.

This is the problem to which this book is devoted. We concentrate on how to get the right information out of the electronic equipment to help the boat win races.

Everyone on board a racing yacht will use the instrument system at some time or another. Tacticians for wind information, helmsman and trimmers for boat speed, mastmen for time to the next sail change. But someone must be responsible for this information, its accuracy, collection, assimilation, comparison to what has gone before and projection into what lies ahead.

We will be concentrating on the equipment that's normally used in the mainstream of yacht racing, what we'd call the instrument system. While radars, autopilots and weather satellite systems all have parts to play in specialised ocean races, they are of little direct consequence to those of us who do not wish, or have no opportunity, to race around the world or across oceans. So we are going to ignore those aspects of the navigator's job.

The modern navigator's role often includes many other responsibilities than the ones we will cover in the book, including all the input and knowledge on the weather situation during the race, paperwork before and during the regatta for entry, protests and much more. We consider all these very important tasks, but we decided to keep the scope of the book very focused on the numbers and the data that are really at the heart of what a navigator does on and off the water.

Development Of This Book

In 1992 Mark wrote the first edition of this book, called *Chisnell on Instrument Techniques*. Two decades later, in 2012 it was updated as *Sail Smart*. This time, we decided not to leave it so long and, working together, we have updated the text.

As a book mostly focused on the theory behind the use of numbers on board (rather than being about the equipment and technology) the text has not aged badly. However, we agreed that there were new aspects of the navigator's role, and the use of numbers, data and information on board a sailboat, that were worth adding.

Electronics systems on board become more advanced and more affordable with every passing year, and learning how to use them and interpret the numbers is key to every modern keelboat sailor who wants to compete. We hope that this new book can help more and more sailors to understand the importance of **mastering data to win**!

Mark Chisnell & Gilberto Pastorella
June 2023

CHAPTER 1

The Role Of The Navigator

MARK: During the period that this book was being rewritten, the British Optimist fleet visited my local sailing club for one of the year's big events. I walked around the dinghy park (with our dog), dazzled by the array of beautifully prepared racing equipment. Afterwards, when I returned to the book, I wondered; how many of those children have ambitions to race bigger boats – keelboats, or yachts? And how many of those want to be the navigator aboard those yachts?

I'd bet a few pounds on the answer being ... zero. Zippo. None. Nil. I'd guess that to the last boy and girl they a) don't know much if anything about the navigator's role, and b) they will all want to steer whatever boat they are racing. However, if they're good enough and they follow a path out of dinghy racing and onto bigger boats, they will soon discover that there are very few sailors driving. There's a lot more doing all the other jobs. And one of the most challenging, interesting, and influential is navigator – but it's also the least understood; even amongst the other crew on a competitive modern racing yacht, the role of the navigator can be something of a mystery.

How many Optimist sailors see themselves becoming navigators?

The output from the navigator's work is obvious enough – the numbers on the yacht's displays are there for anyone to see. Everyone should hear the times to the laylines, waypoints and buoys called out by a navigator who's on their game. Some of the crew will overhear the conversation between the navigator and the tactician on the potential impact of wind or current on the next leg. Those who are in the speed loop will get input from the navigator as they feedback performance data from their computer. The whole crew should listen to the navigator's briefing on the weather before a race, or the debrief after the race, where the navigator might produce data and graphs analysing the yacht's performance. And yet, despite seeing and hearing all this, few of the crew will have any idea about the work that went into delivering all this information.

This is a little strange, given the changes that have taken place in wider society in the last couple of decades. This is the age of big data, some of the world's biggest and most successful companies are now founded on the collection and manipulation of information – of data. Popular books on statistics, decision making and information technology hit the bestseller lists, like Nate Silver's 2012 *Signal and the Noise,* which was Amazon's #1 non-fiction book that year – and essential reading for anyone interested in processing data in any form.

Sailboat racing has not been immune from this transformation; for instance, there are now some excellent data analytics apps that are readily available. This was not the case two decades ago. However, the potential for data analysis and use has perhaps not been as widely absorbed, or as exploited, as it could be. The very first edition of this book was released into a world where putting instrument systems and computers on boats was still an innovation. Now we carry many, many times the computing power of those early onboard systems in the phone in our pocket. The potential for the use of this data to win sailboat races is enormous – and the 'navigator' sits at the very heart of this opportunity.

We said in the introduction that 'navigator' was now something of a misnomer, and perhaps changing the name would help – it does sound a little fusty and old-fashioned. Let's be honest, no cool Oppy kid with the latest shades, a buzzing news feed and Insta or TikTok account is going to be attracted to that job title. Unfortunately, I don't think we're going to start calling the navigator the 'Head of Data and Performance Strategy' anytime soon. But we shouldn't let the name take anything away from what an extraordinary role the modern navigator has aboard a racing boat.

There is no one else so deeply involved in all aspects of the team's performance. Depending on the project, the work can start at the design or purchase stage. What's the boat for? What are the goals of the owner and crew? It might be winning a class at the Copa del Rey in Palma, Cowes Week or Block Island Race Week. It could be winning the ORC or IRC European or World Championships, or one of the offshore classics like the Fastnet or Sydney-Hobart. Perhaps the goal is a major one-design title like the Rolex Swan Cup. Whatever it is, the navigator is the person that will be working with the skipper, project manager or designer to analyse and find the right boat or design for the job.

Next will come the sail package – sail designs need to be tailored to the goals and winning one of those offshore classics is going to require a completely different sail inventory to one developed to win an inshore championship with a predominance of windward / leeward courses. Both of these tasks will require a full analysis of the weather that can be expected at the venues, and that will in turn require an understanding of forecasting, and risk.

The research won't stop with the weather – the navigator will need to understand everything about the wider geography of the racing venues – tides, currents, rocks and shoals, the mountains and plains that form the backdrop to local weather generation. Then, of course, there will be the paperwork – not the most interesting part of the job, but someone has to do it. And good attention to detail for rule compliance at all stages of entry and competition will be essential.

For the lucky ones with a new boat, there will be a brand new instrument system to specify, and lots of research to do into new developments in sensors, displays, processors and software. There will be the electrical and electronics installers to talk to, and layouts to design and finalise. The good navigator doesn't leave anything to chance – if you're the one relying on the accuracy of the compass, then you're the best person to decide where to put it.

When the boat is launched and training or early season racing starts, the navigator can begin

The navigator will be deeply involved in all aspects of the teams performance, be it for an offshore classic, like the Sydney-Hobart race, or a one-design title

the process of calibration, and tailoring the data available on deck to the crew. What follows on the water is the visible part of the job. The navigator is in the thick of the action for every moment, supporting strategic and tactical decision-making, and monitoring all aspects of performance – tactical and speed related – to eliminate weakness and exploit strengths.

Back ashore, there will be data to process, and perhaps a debrief to organise and present. These tasks will absorb all the time and expertise available – and for that reason many of the pro teams at the elite level employ experts to do the analysis for them. Aboard a TP52 or Ocean Race boat, the navigator is at the sharp end of a team of people devoted to improving performance – add management and planning to the 'nice to have' skill set.

We said in the introduction that we wouldn't deal with some aspects of the role – and many of the things we're not going to talk about are part of the tasks that we have just outlined. This book

won't tell you everything you need to know about the navigator's job. What it will do is lift the veil on the core knowledge and techniques required to be a good navigator in the new information age. At the heart of the book, and at the heart of the job is what it takes to get good quality, accurate data on board a racing yacht. This is really what mastering the data is all about – go and read *Signal and the Noise* if you don't believe us.

We've provided some examples of how to use that data on board, and in the final chapter we point to some of the ways this might be expanded in the future, as AI tools are rolled out and become commonplace. Never forget though, that the foundation for everything we can do now and in the future is accurate measurement of wind speed and direction, boat motion, sail shape and power development. And achieving that, as we will see, is not easy – but if you have the motivation, curiosity and skills to master the data, then the opportunities in the sailing world are as wide as a Pacific Ocean horizon.

The navigator needs to know everything about the wider geography of the race venue

CHAPTER 2

The Key Elements Of Data

On Board

There are many different ways to discuss the data on board. This chapter is devoted to helping the reader to understand the logical blocks that he or she has to deal with, and how they are related to each other.

There are three main elements that we will discuss:

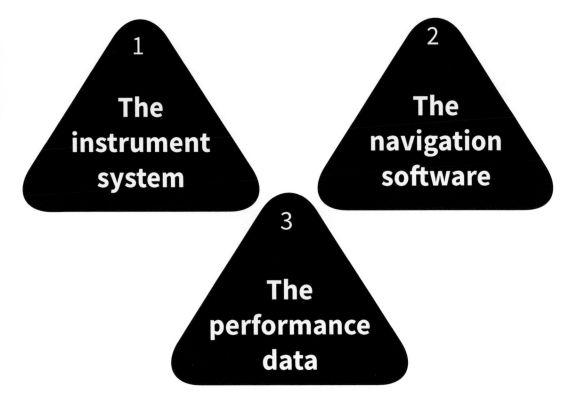

It may seem strange to put an electronic system, a software package (or app) and a package of numbers (data) on the same level, but this distinction will help you during the whole book, and in real life sailing, to have a clear and simple idea on how to work and divide your actions into smaller steps.

Instrument Systems

In the book, the term 'instrument system' means what sailors would normally call an 'electronic system' or just the 'electronics'.

When we talk about instrument systems we have to keep in mind that we are actually talking about the sum of three main constituents parts:

- The **sensors** that measure the physical effects, be it boat speed, apparent wind angle or compass heading
- The **processor** (or 'brain') that translates the raw sensor data into a number we can understand, and does some maths to create new numbers
- The **displays** that communicate these numbers to the world

A wind sensor from A+T Instruments

Everyone else on the boat often just sees the displays, but most of the time, what the navigator has to deal with are the other two parts, the sensors and the processor.

There are dozens of different types of sensors, and many different processors and displays. And new ones come out every year, while existing systems get updated. We will see in the section dedicated to calibration the importance of having good sensors and a good processor that allows you to calibrate the system properly. A key aspect of modern systems is that they allow external components (such as a PC) to be connected to receive or send data to and from the processor. It will be clear why this is important in the next chapter.

Overall, a navigator has to be able to always understand:

- What sensor is measuring what physical attribute of the boat
- Which part is doing 'the maths'
- What the role of the displays is

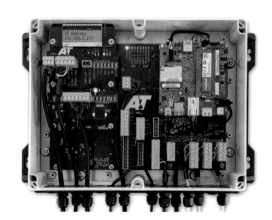

A processor from A+T Instruments

By having this clearly in mind as soon as we jump on the boat, the navigator can work in a much more effective way towards better data and therefore better performance for the team.

A multi-function display from A+T Instruments

INSTRUMENTS

+44 (0)1590 718182 | info@aandtinstruments.com | www.aandtinstruments.com

Superbly Engineered Marine Instruments

A+T makes very high performance and well engineered sailing instrument upgrades for existing yachts as well as complete systems for new-builds and major refits. We also make a complete range of spares, sensors and accessories for legacy instrument systems.

Wind Sensors

Improved replacement for your existing wind sensor and replacement parts.

Processors

Very high performance and wide range of interfaces.

Displays

The toughest, biggest and brightest full colour marine instrument displays.

I can't speak highly enough of A+T, the products and service have been great and it has all worked exactly as advertised on the box – I've no doubt that the instrument upgrade was part of our winning combination for the regatta.

PROCESSORS · AUTOPILOTS · WIND SENSORS · DISPLAYS · CUSTOM PROJECTS · SHUT OFF VALVES & SENSORS · 24HRS CUSTOMER SUPPORT · 5 YEAR WARANTY

Everyone on the boat sees the instrument displays (here from A+T Instruments), but the navigator needs to know about the sensors and processors

For instance, if we know that the boat speed shown on the mast display is coming from the paddlewheel, before being corrected by a calibration table in the processor, and then damped (averaging the data) directly by the mast display (but not the others), then we can work out much more quickly why we are seeing one number on the mast, and a different number on the other displays around the boat.

The three parts (sensors, processor and displays) can be merged into one single piece of kit; in that case, we would call that a **stand-alone unit**. There are more and more of these being developed and sold for small boats and dinghy classes. These allow small boats to have some data. In particular, they usually provide compass, GPS and Gyro (3-axis acceleration) data and allow this to be recorded and analysed once back ashore.

Some of the principles explained in this book also apply to this equipment, but they take no account of the wind speed or direction, nor any current or tidal water flow. Ultimately, you can think of stand-alone equipment as equivalent to a smartphone. It has a display, a GPS, some sensors (usually a compass, a gyroscope) and software to analyse and generate information – but it's hopefully a bit more shockproof and waterproof.

A stand-alone unit from Vakaros

Navigation Software

We said in the previous section that an instrument system can be connected to a PC or an external device. So why is this important?

Instrument systems usually have displays that are built to be outside on a boat (and therefore exposed to the elements), and their interfaces and menus are quite basic as a result and a long way from what we expect from modern software in terms of the user's experience. This is one of the reasons why navigation software has evolved and now more and more racing yachts are running a PC connected to the instrument system.

Overall, we can say that the main functions of navigation software are that it allows:

- The navigator to view all the data that the instrument system on board is calculating (including information that's not shown on the on-deck displays)
- Management of the geometry of the race
- Some extra calculations to generate new insights on the racing

- Management of some key elements of the performance data

In offshore racing, the navigation software is also the tool used to work on weather files, analysis of the optimal route and more, but this is beyond the scope of this book.

Let's get deeper into these groups of functions (leaving the first one, as it is self-explanatory):

Management Of The Geometry Of The Race

Racing around windward / leeward and coastal races means going around marks. The navigation software allows the navigator to have those marks in the system and to be able (thanks to the GPS information received from the boat's electronics) to know everything about the position of the boat compared to the marks, the relative position of the marks to each other and, last but probably most importantly, the position of the marks and the boat relative to the wind (again, thanks to the wind data arriving from the instrument system).

This means that in the navigation software

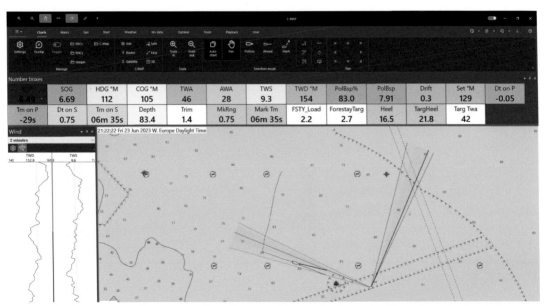

	SOG	HDG °M	COG °M	TWA	AWA	TWS	TWD °M	PolBsp%	PolBsp	Drift	Set °M	Dt on P
	6.69	112	105	46	28	9.3	154	83.0	7.91	0.3	129	-0.05
Tm on P	Dt on S	Tm on S	Depth	Trim	MkRng	Mark Tm	FSTY_Load	ForestayTarg	Heel	TargHeel	Targ Twa	
-29s	0.75	06m 35s	83.4	1.4	0.75	06m 35s	2.2	2.7	16.5	21.8	42	

An example of navigation software output (here from Expedition navigation and sailing software) – the window across the top shows all the key data, bottom left is a two-minute strip plot of the wind, and to the right of it the racecourse, with laylines and chart data

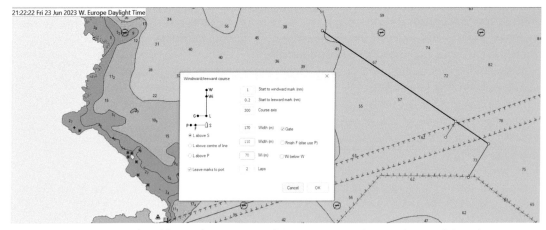

The window to set up a windward-leeward course in Expedition navigation software – the user defines distances between marks and other features of the course

you have windows and buttons that allow you to position the racecourse and other key marks (for example, the start line, no-go zones / boundaries, etc.) and the computing power to know things like:

- The distance to the windward mark
- The distance of the next leg
- The bearing of the next mark

These three examples can all be calculated without the need for wind data. However, we can also work out things like the bias on the start line, or whether the next leg is a reach or a full upwind leg. These last two examples can be calculated because the system also has wind data.

Overall, these functions allow the navigator to quickly set the course, change it on the go, and have (and therefore, be able to give) information on the geometry to the rest of the crew.

Extra Calculations To Generate New Insights On The Racing

A fundamental part of what the navigation software is used for is the calculation of new variables. These are generated using both the instrument data and other inputs that the user feeds

manually into the software before or during the race.

The most important category of input is performance data (aka 'polars'). We will discuss later what a polar diagram is and how it works, but it is important to know that, by mixing performance data and real-time data, navigation software can calculate variables that are at the heart of a navigator's job, in particular:

- Time to burn at the start
- Layline times
- Next leg information

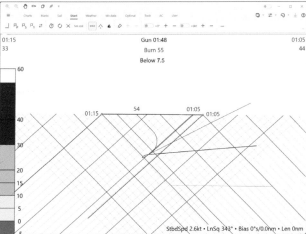

A screenshot of the software showing burn times to both ends of the start line (see page 71 for more detail)

Expedition

navigation and sailing software

In addition to these numbers, lots of navigation software allows the calculation of 'What If?' scenarios. These are basically simulations that allow the navigator to see what happens to the numbers in the previous list if the wind rotates by, say, 10 degrees, or increases by 2 knots, or if the current changes.

The information about the geometry of the course and these extra calculations are usually the numbers that are the soundtrack of the relationship between the navigator and the tactician. Mastering how to read and communicate these is key for the modern navigator.

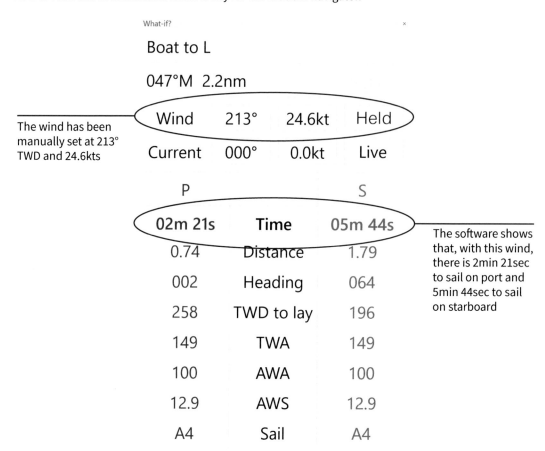

This 'What If?' app shows layline times in the conditions as well as other parameters for the leg. It allows the navigator to input wind direction and speed manually. In this case, the wind was still blowing from 203°, but the navigator had input a manual wind of 213° because a right shift of 10° was expected, and so now the tactician could be told how that shift would change the layline times and other parameters

Managing Elements Of The Performance Data

Polar tables deserve a bigger role in this book than just as a sub-chapter of the navigation software, and we will discuss them in many more chapters, starting from the next one. For now, let's think of them as tables full of numbers that change during the season and even during the day.

Navigation software has an easy interface to manage all this data and to allow us to record data about performance to improve these calculations and their accuracy.

As we discussed in the Introduction, it is important that the navigator always knows where things are calculated and generated. Many processors can, for example, handle performance data (polar tables) within the system without the need of additional navigation software.

Navigation software can (and usually does) send data back to the instrument system to be displayed on the deck displays, for example:

- During the start sequence, many boats display the five-minute countdown on the mast displays
- Or during the race, the trimmers want to know about the target boat speed on the display in the cockpit

The navigation software can also often manage things like calibration tables.

It is very important that the navigator decides where he / she wants to manage the data, and sticks to that. Having the same data in multiple locations or not knowing where things are calculated is the first step towards problems!

This is a familiar and reccurring problem because software and systems often come from different companies, and they are all pushing to develop the same features. These days you can ping the start line using a chart plotter, or even calculate laylines.

The key takeaway is:

Decide a strategy, make sure you know where you want to handle which data, and stick to it

Last, but definitely not least, a very important note. The navigation software is what the navigator is looking at for 50% of the race (the other 50%, he should be looking at what is happening on the water). Some navigators keep up to 30 different variables displayed on their screen. It's a really important skill to establish a configuration for the data and the display that works for you, and that you stick to – speed in manipulating the software and data is crucial to doing the job well. The speed at which you can change a course, create a 'What If?' scenario or find the value of a specific variable, is the speed at which you give the right answer to the tactician waiting for it.

The secondary ability to anticipate these same questions because you can see a situation developing is what makes for a really good navigator.

GILBERTO: More than once I've heard a discussion about navigation software displaying the target boat speed as 7.5kts, while on the deck displays it was showing 7.8kts. In the end, it usually turns out that this is because the navigator and the crew didn't have a clear picture of where the data on the display was coming from, and there was confusion between two different polar tables uploaded in different parts of the system.

There's enough going on without confusion caused by conflicting displays

Performance Data

The third key element that needs to be examined in more detail (as we have already mentioned a few times) is performance data and, in particular, polars.

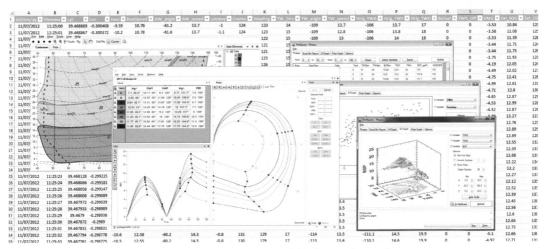

Just some of the multitude of performance data analyses available from SailingPerformance

What Are Polar Tables?

The whole topic of yacht performance and data analysis centres on the polar table.

The polar table gives us a convenient way of recording performance, both graphically and in a table. It takes each wind speed separately and, for every true wind angle, records the boat speed of the yacht. These are then plotted on a polar plot using one line for each wind speed:

- The angle from the vertical representing the true wind angle (TWA), that is, the angle of the wind relative to the heading of the yacht
- The distance from the centre representing the boat speed

Polar Table Accuracy

The usefulness of the polar table is dependent on its accuracy, something we should discuss first.

Many of the reasons for polar table errors will be discussed in the chapter on calibration. Obviously calibrating the system carefully will eliminate as much error as possible. But there is one major difficulty that limits all our efforts which, at the moment, cannot be resolved. That is the problem

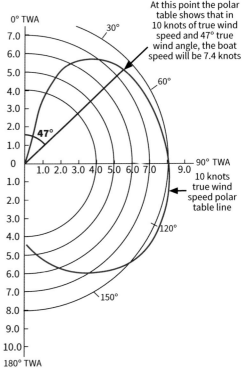

At this point the polar table shows that in 10 knots of true wind speed and 47° true wind angle, the boat speed will be 7.4 knots

A polar table for 10 knots true wind speed

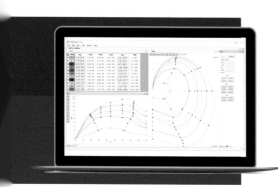

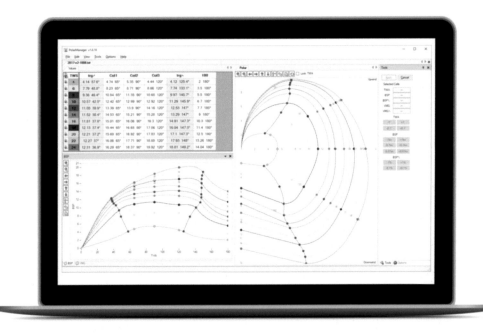

The polar manager app from SailingPerformance

of **wind sheer** and **gradient**.

We said earlier that the polar table measures the boat speed at each particular wind speed and angle. Each point on the table represents the balancing of the water and wind forces on the yacht. The wind speed and angle are measures of the aerodynamic force available, and the boat speed measures the hull's equal and opposite hydrodynamic response.

We can measure the speed of the boat accurately, and we can measure the true wind angle accurately, especially if we define it as half of the angle that the boat tacks through. But we cannot measure the true wind speed as it relates to boat speed. We can measure it at the top of the mast, but if we try to use this number as a measure of the force that the wind is supplying to drive the boat forwards we will fail.

The reason being that the wind can have any value it likes below the masthead, whilst the masthead value stays the same. We could read ten knots at the masthead and be reaching at a cheerful ten knots with a breeze that was ten knots virtually down to the water. Or, we could be sitting becalmed, still recording ten knots at the masthead but with a breeze that stubbornly refused to come any closer to the sails.

How is any polar table based on masthead values of wind speed going to cope with that? The answer is ... it is not. And until we find a significantly better way of measuring the wind power available to the rig and build our polar tables around it, their usefulness will be limited.

That's the bad news; the good news is that, in practice, if you sail at the same venue, in roughly the same weather conditions, be they sea breezes or frontal systems, then the wind velocity gradient will not change that much and you can safely use your polar table. Otherwise, we would not have devoted any space to it in this book! But never consider it cast in stone. As soon as you get a different weather type, or sail somewhere new (like moving from the Atlantic coast to the Mediterranean) you can expect problems. So, the rule is to approach polar tables with a healthy scepticism.

Wind sheer and gradient means the wind may be very different below the masthead compared to what is recorded at the masthead

Velocity Prediction Programs

Velocity prediction programs, or VPPs as they are known, are computer predictions of a yacht's performance. The computer has a model of the design in its memory, which the VPP then analyses to calculate how fast it thinks the yacht will go at different true wind angles and speeds. It does this by calculating the amount of drag the yacht will develop to stop it accelerating, and the amount of drive the rig will generate to push it forward. It then uses the inherent symmetry of sailing to predict the boat speed at which these two forces will balance.

Where the aerodynamic driving force is exactly matched by the hydrodynamic drag, the boat speed is the best that can be achieved for that wind speed and angle. The most obvious use of something like this is in the design process, where VPPs can be used to test and refine designs before they are ever built.

Another use is in some rating systems, where each team enters some information about the boat, the rig, etc. and the system uses a simplified VPP to predict the performance. The rating is then based on the performance profile.

The big advantage of this over a traditional 'single number' rating system is that the boat can be rated differently through the range of conditions to allow for its particular characteristics. So light air flyers get a rating that means they have to fly in light air to win, but equally, does not penalise them for this performance when the breeze is up, making it impossible for them to win in those conditions.

Our interest is whether the polar tables generated by the VPPs can be used for the tactical and performance analysis techniques that occupy the rest of this book. And the answer is a conditional 'yes'.

Whilst all VPPs are not perfect (nor are they equal, a great deal of resource needs to be devoted to developing accurate predictions of yacht performance), they can be a very effective design tool. They can often effectively compare designs and differentiate the one that will be faster in both the real world as well as the computer world. But this does not mean that the actual performance numbers predicted can be directly lifted onto the yacht.

While the VPP may be internally consistent – predicting accurately how much faster the boat will go when you change the true wind angle by 50 degrees – the predictions may not accurately map onto the real world, which is what we require. One aspect of this is the way your boat speed calibration varies with heel angle. The boat speed sensors are measuring the water flow under the hull, which is a function of the boat speed, rather than a direct measurement of it.

If this function alters with the heel angle, then you should have a different calibration for the boat heeled as opposed to upright. While this can

be achieved, it's unusual outside of high budget professional campaigns.

What this means is that while the boat speed reading is consistent from one minute and one day to the next if you are watching it on board, it will vary when compared to an absolute measurement. So, for an identical hull speed through the water, the boat speed might read 10 knots going downwind and 9.8 upwind, because the water flows past the boat speed sensor differently when the boat is heeled to when it is upright.

But because it always reads 9.8 when you are going upwind at that hull speed, the instruments are always consistent with themselves, and it is not a problem when you are sailing. It only becomes a problem when you try to compare your measured figures to VPP figures which have no allowance for the practicalities of your instrument system.

The boat speed readings may be affected by the amount the boat is heeled

Another potential issue is whether leeway is included in the true wind angle calculation in both the VPP and the instruments. We will discuss leeway in more detail later; it is the effect whereby the boat slips as a result of the balance of forces pushing it forwards. It's just worth noting here that for the VPP's predicted wind angles to accurately translate onto the yacht, both instruments and VPP need to assume either that the boat is travelling in the direction it is pointing (normally called the heading) or the direction in which it is moving (normally called the course).

If the answer is different for the VPP and the instruments, then you will need to take this into account when the VPP predictions are used on the yacht, or there will be an error. For instance, if the true wind angles in the VPP are based on heading, then they are going to be narrower than the ones you will measure on the boat if the true wind angle calculation includes leeway and it is calibrated correctly.

We will see that this doesn't matter when it comes to calibrating the true wind angle, but it will help you understand whether the boat's performance is matching the VPP or not.

A bigger problem is due to our rather tiresome friends, wind sheer and gradient. For the VPP to match your sailing numbers on the water you need both an equivalent wind gradient to that assumed by the program, and the wind speed measured at the same height.

Most modern VPPs use a standard height for the wind speed of 10 metres. This is a lot lower than most modern yachts will be measuring (at the masthead), so there's immediately a source of error right there. Fortunately, the differences produced by these problems tend to be in the magnitude rather than in the shape of the polar curves. So the VPP at a given wind speed will produce a polar curve of the same shape as the real data – although all the boat speeds may be either a little higher or a little lower.

All this means that a VPP polar is a good enough place to start the generation of the yacht's polar table. You will certainly have to correct it, but it is likely that the corrections will be of a similar amount and type for much of the table. So, if you can get hold of a VPP for the boat, use it as a start point for performance analysis. But we would not recommend too much reliance on it for exact target boat speeds or tactical techniques until you have had a good opportunity to test it.

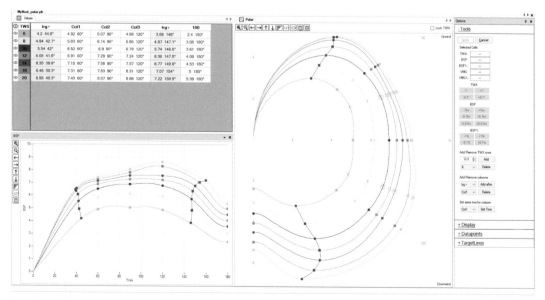

A VPP polar from SailingPerformance

Velocity Made Good & Target Boat Speeds

There are a couple more concepts that we need to discuss when talking about performance.

The first is velocity made good or VMG, which is defined as the boat speed multiplied by the cosine of the true wind angle (see diagram below). It is a measure of how efficiently you are sailing to windward or leeward – it increases if you can sail either closer (if upwind) or wider (if downwind) to the wind at the same speed, or at the same angle to the wind but faster.

We are usually interested in two particular values – the maximum VMG that can be achieved upwind and downwind. These are both numbers that we can find using the polar table.

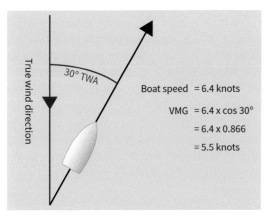

The calculation of velocity made good or VMG

In the diagram opposite, we take a horizontal line (blue), perpendicular to the zero true wind angle line, and move it until it touches the top of the (red) polar table. Then the maximum upwind value of VMG is given by the vertical height up the zero true wind angle line, using the same scale that the boat speed is plotted on (6.9kts).

Equally importantly; the correct boat speed (6.9kts) and true wind angle (37°) to sail for optimum VMG can be read off the polar where the line touches. This speed and angle are known as the target boat speed and target true wind angle for upwind sailing. They are target values because they are the values we must try to sail at to achieve maximum performance upwind.

The same principle is followed for the downwind VMG, target boat speed and target true wind angle (shown here in green).

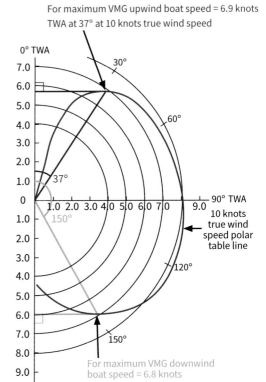

Finding the target boat speed and target wind angle (TWA) from the polar table

We need to understand why you are using a target boat speed when it is the VMG that you are trying to optimise. The problem with VMG is the momentum of the boat. If you sail watching the VMG you will see that the closer to the wind you go, the higher the VMG gets. This is because the true wind angle is getting narrower, but for no corresponding loss of boat speed (initially). The boat is maintaining speed because of its momentum.

So you keep steering closer to the wind and the VMG keeps getting higher, until finally the boat runs out of momentum, and the boat speed comes crashing down, taking the VMG with it. It is this lag in the response of VMG to your sailing angle that has led to the technique of sailing as close as possible to the boat speed which is known to optimise your VMG.

This is best achieved by programming your instruments to display on a dial the target boat speed for the wind speed. Since the target varies as the wind speed goes up and down, having the polar table in the instrument system (and / or in the navigation software, as we will see later in the book) so that it can update the value for you is a big help to the helmsman.

Downwind it is sometimes easier to sail the boat at the true wind angle that matches the target boat speed, rather than aim for the boat speed itself. Many teams also keep the TWA target visible on the displays during the upwind, to give more references to the helmsman and the tactician.

On a free leg where there is no need to tack, the principle is even simpler. Just look up in the polar table the speed you should be achieving at that wind angle and wind speed. This is your target boat speed for the leg.

We must finish with the familiar proviso that all this is dependent on the polar table which is variable according to the wind gradient. So do not set too much store by your targets. If you can beat them easily, do not relax, revise the targets upwards. It is for this reason that we have never really approved of displaying targets for free legs. The best means of sailing the boat at its optimum is simply to race hard against the boats around you. But when you are offshore on your own, or at night, they can certainly help.

For VMG legs their usefulness is well established: the person steering (the 'helm') is better off with something to aim at, though they may well be revising the number they see against what they feel from the boat. It is not unusual to be deliberately sailing two or three tenths above or below your target because of the particular conditions. The helm's 'feel', if they are any good, is a lot more sensitive than the instruments so should not be ignored.

Overall, a good navigator has to be able to balance the work they do to have reliable and realistic polar tables (thanks to data collection and data analysis), and the experience and communication with the helmsman and trimmer to understand why on certain days the numbers are consistently different from the targets.

Use the instruments to help you sail to your target boat speed

The Wind Triangle & Some Nomenclature

As we discussed in the previous chapter, an instrument system uses data from several different sensors, then applies some maths to this original data in order to calculate additional information.

The most important and crucial piece of maths involved is known as the wind triangle, a vector calculation which we are going to look at here. Understanding this is fundamental to having a solid base to understand all the other sections in this book.

The four basic measurements that are made by the system are:

- The **boat speed**, which comes from some form of impeller, paddlewheel or solid state device and is exactly what it says it is – the speed of the boat moving through the water
- The **compass heading**, which is straightforward – the magnetic (or true) heading of the boat
- The **apparent wind speed**
- The **apparent wind angle**

The apparent wind is the breeze that you feel blowing across the boat, i.e. the one that you can directly measure on board. It is the product of three components:

1. The wind blowing across the land – which we will call the **ground wind**, this is the wind that you will see on the weather maps

2. The wind produced by the motion of the water relative to the land – which we will call the **tide wind**, it is equal in strength and opposite in direction to the water flow

3. The wind produced by the motion of the boat relative to the water – which we will call the **motion wind**, it is equal in velocity to the boat speed and blows in 180° opposition to its direction of motion

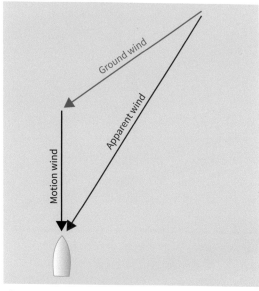

The apparent wind triangle showing the components of apparent wind (simplified – without the tide wind)

The vector product of all three is the apparent wind, which is the only one of these that we can measure directly. But the wind triangle allows us to calculate the rest.

Let us assume for the moment that we have no GPS connected into the instruments and that we are out of sight of the shore, so we have no idea whether the water is moving relative to the land or not. The wind triangle uses the boat speed, apparent wind speed and the apparent wind angle to calculate what we are going to call the true wind angle and speed – the third side of the triangle. These two numbers are a great deal more useful than the apparent wind speed and angle, for lots of reasons that we will see as we continue this book.

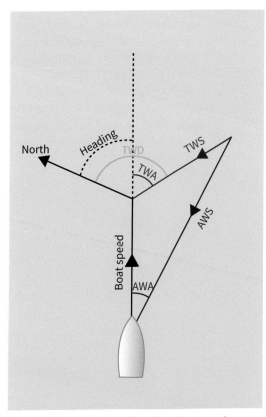

The wind triangle connects heading, boat speed, apparent wind angle (AWA), apparent wind speed (AWS), true wind angle (TWA), true wind speed (TWS) and true wind direction (TWD) (simplified – ignores leeway)

The point we want to stress now is what happens when we relate this true wind angle we have calculated to the fourth measurement that we have made, which is the compass heading. The result that we get is what the instruments usually call the true or magnetic wind direction. It is probably the most useful tactical tool that you have on the boat; because it is calculated independently of the boat's direction, it is the most precise measure you have of the wind shifts that you should be using to sail quickly round the course.

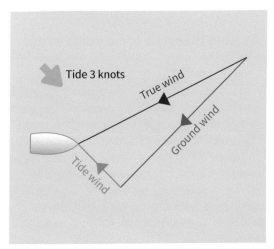

The ground wind and the tide wind combine to form the true wind, whose direction and speed can be calculated from the boat speed, compass, apparent wind speed and angle, as above

The most important point to grasp here is that changes in wind speed and direction that you see on the true wind on the instruments are not just caused by the ground wind altering, they are also affected by the tide / current changing – because of the tide wind component.

The consequences of this fact cannot be underestimated. We will start with an extreme example: let's consider a cross tide beat where the tide changes. There is no question that, if you have a tide running across a beat, the tack that puts the tide under your leebow will take you a lot closer to the mark than the one which puts it on the weather bow.

The reason this is such an advantage lays in the basics of the wind triangle we have just explained. The tack where the tide is under your leebow is lifted due to the tide wind component. If you sail on the other tack then you are sailing on a header that will disappear when the tide changes. This is why you tack when the tide goes round – so you are always sailing on the lift in the true wind created by the tide.

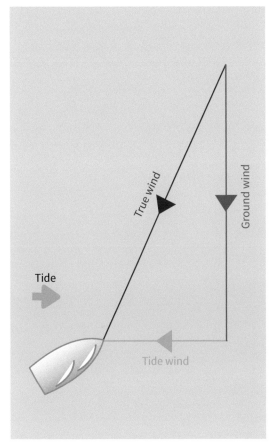

Weather bow tide: True wind headed and strengthened

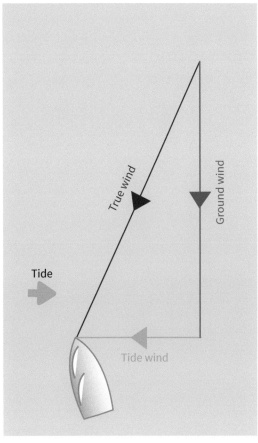

Lee bow tide: True wind lifted and strengthened

One place that you see tidal dependence of the true wind a lot is the Solent.

A typical situation is sailing upwind beside the shore while dodging an adverse tide; as you sail out of the shallow water and into the stronger tide on port tack, the introduction of the tide wind component will cause the true wind on the instruments to head by ten degrees.

Watch out for the jib lifting and the helm coming down as the helmsman accounts for the header. Then when you sail back into the shore on

starboard and out of the adverse tide, you will be lifted again.

This is why it is so important to distinguish between ground and true winds – if the wind effect you saw on the last lap was caused by the tide wind, and the tide has now changed, then it is no good going looking for the same effect again. Equally, if you know the tide will change while you are on an upwind or downwind leg, then get on the lifted tack now, before the tide changes and the lift disappears.

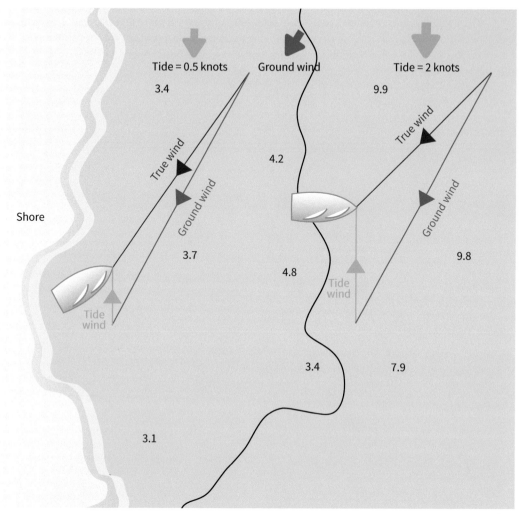

Tide = 0.5 knots   Ground wind   Tide = 2 knots
3.4   9.9
True wind
Ground wind
Shore
3.7   9.8
4.2
4.8
Tide wind
Tide wind
3.4   7.9
3.1

The true wind is going right (looking forward towards the bow) and decreasing in speed as you sail into the stronger weather bow tide

Even the venues where the tidal effect is weaker, like the Mediterranean or Caribbean, this effect has to be considered when sailing in areas where you can find current.

Much the same can be said of what is called the true wind speed. The true wind speed will go up and down with the tide. If the tide wind is increasing your true wind speed, then use it tactically before it (i.e. the tide) changes, to cross a patch of rough water perhaps.

Instrument systems are able to calculate the tide / current in real time by using five inputs:

- Boat speed
- Heading
- SOG (Speed Over Ground)
- COG (Course Over Ground)
- Leeway

We have already defined what boat speed and heading are. SOG and COG are numbers coming from onboard GPS and are defined as Speed Over Ground and Course Over Ground. This means that we are not referring to the water anymore, but to the ground or earth.

We have already mentioned leeway, and it will be discussed further later. It is a key element that allows the system to know if you are going sideways because that's what most boats do, as a result of the physics.

Now that we have some basic definitions of the variables and the geometry involved, it is time to look closer into how to make all these numbers more accurate on our boat.

Calibration

Some Comments On The Calibration Process

Three things should be said about the calibration of yacht instruments.

Firstly, the importance of doing it at all. Any instrument system is only as good as its calibration. You can spend a fortune on the best equipment, but if you do not get out there and set it up properly you might as well not bother. In fact you are probably worse off than you would be with just a compass on board.

In the box below, Mark describes an occasion when the instruments weren't much help. What slowly became clear was that the wind direction was different on each tack. Not only that, but the size of the error varied with the wind speed, and finally the system was set up with such a value of damping that in a down speed tack the instruments were not settling to the correct value before tacking back anyway. All these are things that can be corrected by preparation – so don't skip on it.

Secondly, you must approach the calibration in a very systematic order. Everything in the system is interdependent and if you start calibrating in the wrong order you are wasting your time.

To see why this is so we should look at the wind triangle we discussed in the last section. We can see that much of the key information provided by the instruments, such as the true wind data, is derived from the measurement of only four values: the boat speed, the compass heading, the apparent wind speed and angle. (In fact there is a fifth, the heel angle, but how this is involved we will leave till later.)

If you start to calibrate one of the functions that is calculated from these numbers, such as the true wind angle, before you have calibrated all of its constituent measured values, like the boat speed, then subsequently calibrating the boat speed will upset all the work you have done on the true wind angle.

So the rule is; calibrate every sensor that measures something directly on the boat first and, only when you are completely happy, move onto whatever calibrations are provided for the other functions.

MARK: My first experience with instruments was aboard 12 Metres in the 1987 America's Cup in Fremantle. After a startling promotion from compound sweeper to navigator I stepped aboard for the first day's sailing. Scarcely had I switched the instruments on than we were in the middle of a major down-speed tacking duel, by which I mean that the boat is spun back into the next tack before it has picked up the lost speed from the last one. There seemed to be a lot to do, winding runners, watching layline proximity and checking the shifts. I decided to concentrate on the wind so that I could at least answer the most obvious question 'are we up or down?' quickly.

After five or six tacks I had come to the conclusion that the wind direction I was watching on the dial bore about as much relevance to the wind blowing over the water as it did to the odds of us winning the America's Cup. The result was that, with several tens of thousands of pounds worth of equipment at my disposal, I was completely unable to work out whether we were headed or lifted – not an impressive start.

The phrase 'whatever calibrations are provided for the other functions' brings up an interesting limitation of this book. That it must talk in general terms about something that is specific to the individual reader, i.e. the instrument system itself.

It is a limitation that is going to be most apparent in this section on calibration. Because instrument systems provide the same data, advice on how you use it can be general – but the calibration arrangements are specific. For the values measured by the sensors this is not too much of a problem, the manual will tell you which buttons to press and there are plenty of general points to be made about what you are trying to achieve, and the pitfalls to avoid. The problem arises most acutely with respect to the functions calculated by the wind triangle.

Some of you will have systems that provide no calibration facilities for these numbers at all; others will have functions such as mast twist and upwash, or perhaps direct control over the true wind data itself. Ultimately though, whatever the system, the problem of calibrating it is the same. Our hope is that explaining the problem will help you approach 'whatever calibrations are provided for the other functions' with a clearer view of what you are trying to achieve with them, and how they are supposed to help.

The **third** and final point is that calibration is not a one-time task: you never finish the job. The main reason for this is the phenomena of wind sheer and gradient, which we will discuss in the section on apparent wind speed and angle. But don't forget that all the sensors on the boat are mechanical devices that can be moved, bashed, jarred or kicked, from one week to the next. The instruments are never completely above suspicion, but equally when you are confident that they are right, you can learn from even the strangest readings – as we will see.

Calibration Of The Compass

It is always dangerous to generalise, but it's probably safe to say that most instrument systems 'generally' use solid-state compasses.

There are some different compass technologies available, such as GPS Heading Systems and Fibre Optic Gyros, but pricing keeps these sensors beyond the reach of most of the teams, for now.

The solid-state compass measures the magnetic field strength around it and so detects the direction of north. This signal is much easier to convert and input into a digital instrument system, than the direction of the swinging needle of a conventional compass.

Until the late eighties compass calibration was done by a specialist. A man (usually) would come and tell you, at least on most stripped-out racing boats, that you were a degree or two out here and there and then, usually, leave it at that.

Technology has intervened and provided much greater accuracy. The innovation we have in mind is the autoswing facility, which allows the compass, if certain conditions are met, to calculate its own deviation card and then correct the errors out.

The way these compasses work is to measure the total field strength surrounding them as they turn through a circle. The total field strength measured has two components, one is due to the earth, and the other is from the magnetic fields within the boat – all the magnetic sources that create deviation.

These two fields are fixed relative to different points of reference. The earth's field is fixed relative to the earth and so the yacht rotates within it. Whereas the deviating fields are fixed to the yacht and therefore rotate with the compass as the yacht turns. Because of this difference the compass is able – using some maths that we will not explain as it is quite advanced – to separate them out and so calculate the deviating field. Once it has done this it applies the necessary corrections at all points of the compass.

To make all this happen you usually have to turn the boat in a steady circle or figure of eight, so that the compass can make its measurements, calculations and corrections. This perhaps sounds simpler than it can turn out to be in practice. There are many stories of people struggling to swing compasses; trying on calm days, with no sea state and still failing.

Last, but not least, the auto-swing doesn't calibrate one important part, which is the orientation. You still have to measure if there is an offset between what the compass thinks is the bow, and your actual bow. This may be due to the installation of it not being 100% straight.

The usual way to do this is by comparing the heading with the COG in a no-current situation going straight under engine. Alternatively, comparing it with a different compass brought on board for the occasion is another option.

> MARK: In one particular instance we managed to swing the compass under engine without any issues, but as soon as we went sailing the compass heading would lift by 10 degrees.
>
> We looked at where the compass was installed: low down, on the centreline in the owner's cabin. There were no high voltage cables, tool bags or radios around it, and yet we still had this problem. The heading when motoring was perfect, but under sail it was out. After much head scratching we concluded the only difference was the prop shaft was turning. And when we looked on the yacht's drawings, we found that the compass was mounted only 50cm from the turning prop shaft. We reinstalled the compass further away from the prop shaft, swung it again and lo and behold, everything was fine.
>
> This problem had been caused by the magnetic field of the spinning propeller shaft, creating a constant disturbance in the compass during calibration. As soon as the engine was out of gear and the propeller stopped turning, the magnetic disturbance disappeared. The lesson was that autoswing compasses will autoswing, but only up to a point – the rules about large magnetic fields being placed near them still apply.

Calibration Of The Boat Speed

Today, most boats are equipped with paddlewheel sensors. These are mechanical devices that rotate at a frequency proportional to the speed of the water flowing past them. If they are properly maintained they are extremely reliable; however, they are susceptible to fouling and should be cleaned regularly, then carefully replaced to ensure the sensor lines up with the centreline.

Paddle sensor from A+T Instruments

Boat speed calibration should be one of the first jobs for any new boat, or at the beginning of the season. If you allow the helmsman and trimmers to get used to one boat speed setting, then decide to re-calibrate, they will find it difficult to adjust to the new readings. So it is important that you calibrate as early, and as accurately, as possible.

Every instrument system has its own methods for actually doing the calibration, be it just pressing buttons at the beginning and end of each run or using the trusty calculator. Whatever the specific technique required for the instruments (which you will find in the manual – yes, read it!) there are some general rules that can be followed to get a more accurate result.

1. Always steer as straight a line as possible between your chosen distance marks. If it is a proper measured mile (they are few and far between these days) then the chart will provide the bearing to steer between the transits. If you have worked out the run yourself, then decide on what you are going to steer to and stick to

it. If you waver from the straight line, then the log will measure extra distance that will not be accounted for in the calibration calculation and give you an error.

2. You should choose a time when the water is flat. The log measures the water flow past it, and it is not too choosy whether the flow is created by the boat moving forward or up and down. If the boat is pitching it will record more distance than you have actually travelled. So pick a calm day and, just as importantly, a time when there is not too much traffic about. Not only does the pitching from wash affect the calibration, but there is nothing more infuriating than having to alter course from your fixed bearing to dodge another boat halfway through your final run, and so ruining the entire calibration.

3. Do the runs at fixed engine revs to keep the speed consistent. When you turn around at the end of the run, the boat will slow down because of the braking effect of the turn. It is important that the turn is sufficiently wide so that the boat has accelerated again by the time you start the next run – otherwise the acceleration will affect the results.

Vertical masthead wind sensor from A+T Instruments

Calibration Of The Apparent Wind Speed & Angle

Measuring Apparent Wind Speed & Angle

Apparent wind speed and angle are measured using a masthead anemometer or masthead unit. Their calibration problems are connected, which is why we are dealing with them together.

Development of the masthead unit has concentrated on reducing the weight and windage – critical at the top of the mast – and finding the right position in the air flowing past the boat.

It was way back at the 1987 Fremantle America's Cup that masthead units started to appear in different places: going upwards, outwards, fore and aft from the masthead, and even being moved down to the hounds by the Italia syndicate. By the 2010 America's Cup, when we saw two multihulls racing each other, the wind vanes were located at the top of the mast and on poles at the back of either hull. In the 2021 America's Cup, the sensors were on the bow at the end of the prodder or bowsprit.

The idea behind all this is to move the measuring units to a position where they are least affected by aerodynamic errors and can give the user the most relevant wind information. These errors are created by the deflection of the airflow by the sails. We can see that the apparent wind is altered from that which is created by the pure motion of the boat in the true wind.

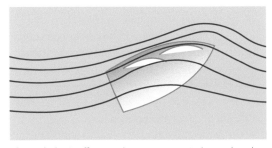

The sail plan's effect on the apparent wind speed and angle can be seen here

The easiest way to understand this is to imagine a motorboat travelling beside a sailing boat at exactly the same speed and angle in a completely uniform wind. If you measured the apparent wind on the motorboat and on the sailing boat, using the instruments on a pole ten feet off the deck, the results would be different. The difference, both in angle and in speed, is due to the deflection of the wind by the sails. Matters can be improved by putting the instruments on top of the mast and raising them as high as possible vertically to get them into clean airflow.

This has the downside that a physical error will be introduced to the angle measurement because the masthead unit twists when the mast tip twists. There is another physical error introduced by the heel of the boat: the speed sensors are measuring the airflow whilst tilted at an angle to it. Although this can be corrected with a relatively simple calculation, it is probably easier and no less accurate to lump it in with all the other errors involved, and deal with them all together. Having done that, how do we go about correcting them?

Where To Make The Corrections

We are going to recommend what might – at first – seem a strange way of calibrating these effects out of the apparent wind speed and angle.

We are going to recommend that we ignore these effects and accept the errors as part of the measurement. So we define the apparent wind angle and speed that we measure and use on a sailboat as including the deflection of that wind by the sail plan.

This makes calibration of these numbers straightforward, but moves the problem down the line to the calibration of the true wind angle and the true wind direction.

We believe the advantage that this approach has is that the problem is more easily and simply dealt with when you are calibrating the true wind. The reason is that the errors caused by deflection of the wind by the sail plan show up much more readily in the true wind than they do in the apparent wind.

If you had a boat with just apparent wind speed and angle sensors you would never know that the

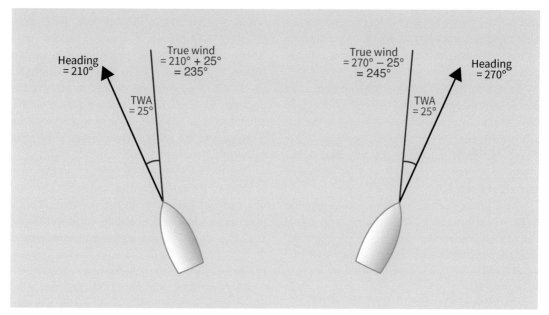

Errors in the apparent wind angle mean that the true wind angle (TWA) is calculated to be too narrow. Although the boat tacks through 60°, 2 x TWA = 50°. This means that the calculated true wind is too far left on starboard tack and too far right on port tack from the actual value of 240°

apparent wind was anything other than correct. Your only real comparison point for the apparent wind angle is whether or not it is the same on both tacks and, once you have set this up, there is little more that you can do. With the apparent wind speed there is even less: you have nothing to compare your measurement to – so you simply trust to the manufacturers and leave it.

But, as soon as you put on board the means of calculating the true wind, then the defects become obvious. If the apparent wind is too narrow, or too wide, on both tacks, then the true wind angle calculated will also be too narrow or too wide. Even this would not matter much ... except that the true wind angle is used with the compass course to calculate the true wind direction. If the angles are wider or narrower than they should be, the true wind will not meet in the middle – it will be different from tack to tack. Suddenly the defects in your calibration become all too clear.

However, it would be very difficult to calibrate the true wind angle, by adjusting the apparent wind angle. We are not aware of any modern systems that use this method. It takes a lot of practice to be able to adjust one number, which only indirectly effects a second, to set up the second number precisely.

So the solution is to leave the apparent wind alone, and not worry about the errors induced by the sail plan. After all, it is no less useful because it is a few degrees bigger or smaller, so why not leave the correction till you get to the true wind angle, where it is important, and it can be calibrated directly and simply?

We will have more of this later when we come on to true wind calibration. It's also worth noting that the top end instrument systems 'back calculate' the apparent wind angle using a calibrated true wind angle – but that's something for the pros to worry about.

Doing The Calibrations

Calibrating the **apparent wind speed** could hardly be easier. We have already mentioned that there is no possible way of comparing it to any other measurement of the apparent wind speed on the boat, so you calibrate it to the manufacturer's value and leave it at that. For those with the resources and the inclination the only alternative is to take the unit off the boat and put it in a wind tunnel to check its measurement against a known wind speed. Some of the manufacturers provide this service for their units at a quite reasonable cost.

Unfortunately, the matter is not quite so simple for the **apparent wind angle**. The goal here is to correct the apparent wind angle so that it is symmetrical. This is complicated because of phenomena that we have already discussed – wind sheer and gradient.

The basic phenomenon of **wind sheer** comes from the physics of moving fluids, they slow down when they come into contact with the friction of a solid. In this case the moving fluid is the air, flowing around the earth, and the wind is increasingly slowed as it nears the ground. This is termed wind velocity gradient – the different velocity of wind at different heights.

The slowing of the air is accompanied by a change in direction. In the Northern Hemisphere the increasing friction rotates its direction anti-clockwise. In the Southern Hemisphere the friction rotates it clockwise – but in all further references to this effect we will assume we are north of the Equator. We've already mentioned that this is what we call wind sheer. None of which would be a problem to the instruments if it was always the same, but of course it is not.

The friction of the wind moving over the earth is not the only reason that the direction of the wind changes with height. It can also be altered by the way the air has mixed. Sometimes this will negate the effect of the friction, and even overwhelm it, so that the wind higher up is to the left (looking upwind) compared to the wind lower down.

So how does this affect the apparent wind angle? When we calibrate it, what we are trying to do is to get the unit to read zero when it is pointing up the centreline of the boat. So that, whether we are on starboard tack or port tack, if the angle

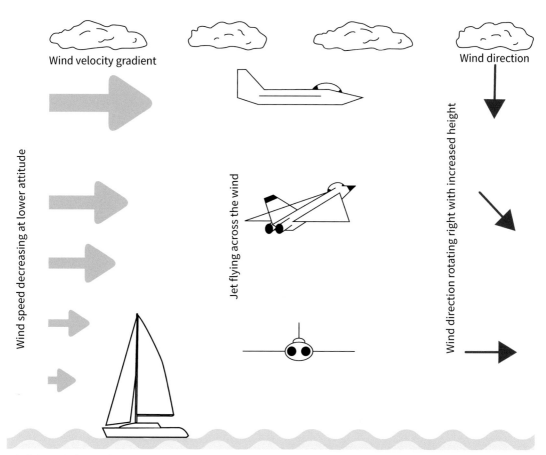

Wind velocity gradient

Wind direction

Wind speed decreasing at lower attitude

Jet flying across the wind

Wind direction rotating right with increased height

Wind sheer: in the Northern Hemisphere wind direction veers (or goes right) with increased height; south of the equator it backs (or goes left)

we are sailing to the wind is the same then the apparent wind angle reads the same.

Wind sheer confuses this considerably – most obviously because the apparent wind angle will not be the same all the way down the mast. The sails will have to be set to some kind of average wind that is over the whole sail plan, and the angle at the top of the mast need not bear any relation to this average sailing angle.

If the wind is rotated anti-clockwise as it gets nearer the ground, then what we will see is wider apparent wind angles on starboard than on port, when to all intents and purposes we are sailing at the same apparent wind angle as far as everything else on the boat is concerned.

We can only deal with this by calibrating the

apparent wind angle when there is no, or at least very little, wind sheer. The idea is to leave it fixed at this calibration even when there is wind sheer. Although the numbers seem crazy, it is better to know that the instruments are right and that you are looking at a physical effect than to be constantly trying to change the instruments to match a fickle wind.

Now we have a chicken and egg situation – we need to be able to tell whether or not there is wind sheer so we can calibrate the instruments – without having the instruments to tell us.

The critical factor in the amount of wind sheer and gradient is the vertical mixing of the layers of air. If the air is turbulent then fast-moving air from above will be mixed with the ground level wind, and there will be little wind sheer or gradient, or possibly it will even be reversed. However, if the air is not turbulent, then there is little vertical mixing, and nothing to prevent the air closer to the ground from being slowed and changing direction.

So what causes this mixing? The answer is usually some kind of thermal effect; the air near the ground is heated by the land (heated in turn by the sun) and so it rises. When it rises it cools again, and drops back down to lower levels. This mechanism mixes up the air. Another method is mechanical turbulence, which occurs as the air flows across hilly or rough ground. Trees, buildings or mountains, or even rough seas, will all start the air rotating and mixing.

We need to know the physical signs of these types of mixing so we can pick a good day to calibrate. In the case of thermal mixing, it is relatively easy; cumulus clouds are created by the rising hot air, giving us some unmistakeable evidence of mixing. Mechanical mixing is a little more difficult to spot, but any weather system wind that is accompanied by clouds or a frontal system will usually be well mixed. This is because it has usually been travelling for some time across sea or land. The days you want to avoid are those high pressure days, when there are either uniform clouds or a clear sky, often accompanied by light winds.

There are other signs you can use as well, associated with the boat. The wind sheer and gradient will make the boat feel different on port tack to starboard. If this is a 'friction' sheer, then you will be able to sail more quickly on starboard tack, with the sails set with looser top leeches. On port tack speed will be much more difficult to get and the sails will need tight upper leeches. The reason is the change in direction of the wind with height. If the wind is rotating to the left (looking forward) as it gets closer to the ground on starboard, so the wind angle is wider at the top than it is low down – hence loose upper leeches and plenty of power; whereas on port the top of the sail will be at a wind angle that is actually too tight – hence stalled and low power sails with tight leeches. (Opposite in the Southern Hemisphere.)

Look out for these signs and do not calibrate when you see them. Check out the 'Don't Panic' section too, to see how you can make use of this information.

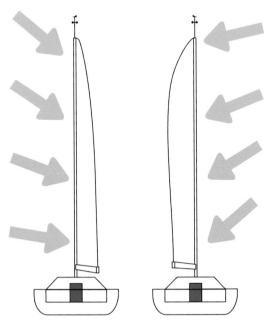

The effect of wind sheer on sail trim: starboard tack with open top leeches and port tack with tighter top leeches – and vice versa in the Southern Hemisphere

Cumulus clouds indicate mixing of the layers of air

When you have chosen your day to calibrate, the routine is simple enough:

- First off, sail the boat head to wind: having the mainsail up will make it easier to tell when this is the case. The apparent wind angle should read zero, if it does not then reset the calibration so it does.
- Next, set the boat up on starboard tack so that it feels comfortable. Make a note of the trim of the sails and the boat speed that you are sailing at. Watch the wind angle for a while and take readings so that you can average them out to a single apparent wind angle number for that tack.
- Then tack the boat over onto port and set her up in exactly the same way – same trim and the same speed.

The idea is that if these things are equal then you are sailing at the same apparent wind angle; in which case the apparent wind angle reading should be the same as well. Watch it for a while and average the numbers. If you have a PC with navigation software connected to the instrument system, then it's likely that it will have the facility to record and average your readings during the procedure.

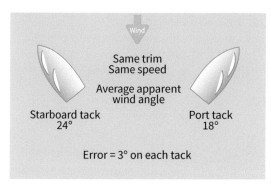

Starboard tack
24°

Port tack
18°

Same trim
Same speed

Average apparent
wind angle

Wind

Error = 3° on each tack

Apparent wind angle calibration

If you have done the head to wind test properly, then the apparent wind angles should be close to the same. But the tack to tack test is more accurate, so if the calibration needs adjusting a little bit, go ahead and do it. Keep repeating the exercise until

you are confident that the apparent wind angle readings are the same on both tacks.

Something to watch out for is the sea state: if it is different on the two tacks then even though you are sailing at the same speed you will not be at the same wind angle – take care.

Calibration Of The Depth

The depth is one of the more straightforward calibrations. This is partly because it is not connected to any of the other measurements through the wind triangle, and partly because there is a fixed measurement to calibrate it to – the depth of the water.

But, having said that, the depth can be a rather fuzzy distance if it is a muddy bottom, so try to find a solid seabed to do it on. The best method is to use a lead line when the boat is in the dock. Measure the depth and then set the datum up so that the depth sounder reading matches it.

Depending on whether you prefer to read actual depth or the water under the keel you will need to include the distance from the face of the depth sounder sensor to either the bottom of the keel or the waterline. So you will need to know this distance, or measure it while the boat is out of the water.

One thing to watch out for is that depth sounders sometimes have trouble getting clear readings in crowded marinas. So if it is reading erratically in any way, wait till you get a calm day and do it whilst you are stopped somewhere outside the marina.

Depth sensor from A+T Instruments

MARK: It's impossible to be too careful when it comes to calibration – there's always a new mistake to make … My most recent came while navigating a forty-footer in the Solent, after we'd swopped an old processor unit out and replaced it with a new one. I was down at the boat on the Friday afternoon before the weekend's racing to check the install, and make sure everything was working and ready. I switched it on, it all fired up, and the numbers all made sense – good to go, I thought, and (a little pressed for time, but that's not really a good enough excuse) I headed off.

The breeze on the Saturday was a northerly, and we spent the day racing in deep water back and forth across the main channel and, although the wind calibrations needed some work, everything worked well enough. By Sunday, the breeze had shifted to the east, and we were now racing along the mainland shore, starting upwind into a foul tide. We came off the leeward end of the line on starboard and headed for the beach where we expected both tidal relief and the benefit of a windshift. The majority of the fleet was to windward of us, and the focus was on calculating an accurate time to the port tack layline, as we would be sailing back out into deep water and foul tide.

The layline call needed to be right, but I wasn't confident in the wind calibrations so I was very focussed on that problem. I had an uneasy feeling in the background though, something didn't quite make sense. I wasn't sure how much water there should be, but the depth under the keel didn't seem to match what I was seeing on the chart.

In the Solent, when racing windward / leeward courses I rarely calculate how much water there should be, instead I rely on the depth sounder. The strategy is to sail into shallow water until the depth sounder reads whatever value is appropriate for the circumstances, and then tack or gybe away. If we have a big lead and are heading towards rocks that value might be as much as a metre as there's no need to take a risk. If we are fighting for every inch in a foul tide with a big bunch of boats on a mud / sand shore it might be just 0.1m, as the extra risk is worth it.

On this occasion, the depth reading on the display was telling me there was nothing to worry about with over five metres of water under the keel. That didn't tie in with either the chart, or the visual and at this point, I should have stopped everything else I was doing and figured out what was going on, but … There was a lot of other things to think about – in particular whether I was giving the tactician (Ian Walker – who kindly provided the Foreword for this book despite this cock up!) the right time to the layline.

BANG!

We went hard aground, so hard aground that we eventually had to be towed off the beach, and retired from the rest of the day's sailing to check the boat out. The calibration numbers had all been transferred by the electronics engineer that had done the installation of the new processor, and the sign on the depth calibration had been switched. An easy enough mistake to make, but the consequences were big, with the display telling us we were completely safe, when in reality we were sailing along with a few centimetres of water under the keel.

The lesson was that when alarm bells are ringing in your head because something doesn't quite make sense in the numbers, pay attention. And don't go sailing until you have checked everything, over and over again.

Calibration Of The Heel Angle

Heel angle is usually calculated by a sensor that measures both heel and pitch.

Although heel angle does not have a direct impact on the wind triangle calculation, it is used in the calculation of leeway (see leeway section below), and leeway is sometimes then used in the calculation of the true wind direction. But even if you are not sure whether this is the case, if your system has heel angle it would pay to calibrate it at the same time as boat speed, compass and apparent wind, i.e. before calibrating the true wind.

The calibration is straightforward. On a calm day set the boat up with slack warps in the dock and put all the gear in its normal sailing position – including the boom and the spinnaker pole (if you have one) on the centreline. Whoever stays on board should also stand on the centreline while they read the heel meter. Under these conditions the heel angle should read zero; if it does not, then adjust it until it does, either with a software calibration or, if one is not provided, by moving the unit itself. The same for the pitch angle.

More and more boats today install gyroscopes. These allow the processors to receive not only the information on heel and pitch, but also heel rate (or roll rate), pitch rate and yaw rate. These measurements of acceleration are used by advanced systems to adjust the wind calculation. Therefore, making sure the system is correctly reading these numbers (be careful with the axis definition and signs – plus or minus – in the systems) is key.

Overall, make sure that the 0 is 0 and that when heeling on port and on starboard the sign is correct for how the processor takes it.

Calibration Of Leeway

The topic of leeway has already come up a couple of times: the sideways slip of a yacht to leeward. It is another function, like the true wind, that is calculated from measured data.

The formula used may vary from one instrument system to another (and fixed-keel monohulls have a completely different formula compared to canting-keel or foiling boats). It will almost certainly depend on boat speed and heel and should be quoted somewhere in the manual. Let us assume that it is as follows:

$$L = (K \times H) \div (Bs \times Bs)$$

where L = Leeway angle
K = Leeway coefficient
H = Heel
Bs = Boat speed

The heel angle and the boat speed can be measured directly by the instrument system; the calibration number we need to find is actually the leeway coefficient. There is an easy way and a hard way to do this.

The easy way is to ask the yacht's designer the value of the leeway coefficient; the hard way is to try to measure it. Somewhere in the middle lies a short cut which involves taking a guess at it, and then watching the leeway angle calculated by the instruments while you are sailing, and checking to see how it matches the design predicted figures. This may not sound very thorough, but the measurement of the leeway coefficient is so difficult that it's probably as good a way as any.

If you do want to try to measure the leeway coefficient, then the goal is to measure the leeway angle for a particular heel angle and boat speed. Knowing these three numbers you can rearrange the above formula to give you the leeway coefficient, like so:

$$K = (L \times Bs \times Bs) \div H$$

The problem arises when you actually try to measure the leeway angle. The diagram below shows how it is supposed to work. You pick a day with around ten to fifteen knots of wind, steady in direction, with reasonably flat water. Then sail upwind on a steady bearing recording the boat speed and heel angle as you go … so far so good.

You now throw a marker out of the back of the boat (something biodegradable rather than plastic). Stand near the mast and, using a hand-bearing compass, take a bearing down the centreline towards the stern. From the same position take a bearing of the marker you dropped overboard. The difference between the two is the leeway angle.

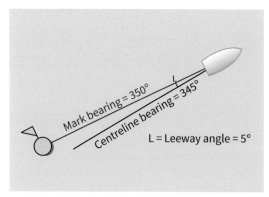

Measuring the leeway angle

This is combined with the boat speed and heel angle that you have been recording to calculate the coefficient. It goes without saying that the flatter the water and the steadier the breeze the easier this is, and even then it is not easy.

Usually, the suggestion is to take a stab at the coefficient, and then adjust it so that the leeway angle that the instruments calculate matches the one provided by the designer – and if you don't have that number, then three degrees of leeway sailing upwind in about 10 knots of true wind speed and flat water won't be too far off.

Calibration Of The True Wind

The calibration of the true wind is something that we have already discussed within the section on apparent wind calibration. We would certainly recommend that you read that before going any further here. Another section that you should look at is the one on the wind triangle (page 35).

Briefly, what we already know is that the true wind speed and angle and the true wind direction are all calculated using the wind triangle, using values of the boat speed, compass, apparent wind speed and angle that come from the sensors.

One subtle issue is whether the true wind angle calculation includes leeway; in other words, is the difference between the wind direction and the boat's heading (the direction the boat is pointing), or the boat's course (which includes leeway)? It's more accurate and consistent to include leeway, as long as leeway is calibrated accurately. However, the method that we are going to use to calibrate the true wind will work whether leeway is included or not.

So, our starting point for true wind calibration is that the boat speed, compass, apparent wind speed and angle are all calibrated correctly. And if the instruments include it in the true wind angle calculation, then leeway also needs to be accurately set up. Once all this is done, the instrument system will probably work perfectly adequately in every respect except two:

- The true wind speed will read differently when you are sailing upwind compared to when you are sailing downwind
- The true wind direction – which is the main tactical tool that the instruments provide you with – will read differently from one tack to the other, and from one sailing angle to another

The reason for this is that the masthead unit is prevented from measuring the apparent wind speed and angle accurately. A couple of factors combine to cause this, the principle one being the deflection of the wind by the sail plan (often called upwash), but twisting of the masthead unit by the mast is also a factor. So much we already know.

We have decided to leave these errors in the measurement of the apparent wind speed and angle, because they are invisible in these numbers. But when the wind triangle calculates the true wind speed and angle we know the errors will reappear. Let's take the case of the true wind speed first.

We consistently find that the **true wind speed** reads higher when sailing downwind compared to sailing upwind. This is presumably because the airflow is accelerated past the masthead unit by the action of the sail to a greater extent downwind, compared to upwind.

Whatever the reason, the effect is consistent. To

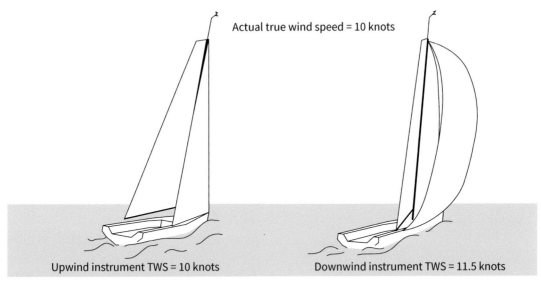

Actual true wind speed = 10 knots

Upwind instrument TWS = 10 knots   Downwind instrument TWS = 11.5 knots

The masthead acceleration effect when sailing downwind

correct it you need to take about 15% off the values of the true wind speed that you see downwind. Some systems, instruments and computers, allow you to do this in a table, so that the correction is always made for you. If your instrument system does not have this facility, you will have to do the correction yourself each time the boat is about to turn a corner.

Note that this error will also exist in the apparent wind. But because the apparent wind is so different upwind compared to downwind, it is almost impossible to spot the effect.

It is important to highlight that there is also a difference in acceleration depending on the headsail being used. For example, sailing an A2 at hot angles or sailing a Code 0 at low angles will generate a completely different flow of air at the top of the rig. Most professional teams have different correction tables for each sail; but this is really the top 1% of the sailing world. But keep it in mind if you sail with different sails at the same angle in the same conditions.

The **true wind angle** is not quite so straightforward. The reason for this is that the combination of errors that are present at the top of the mast cannot be relied upon to produce a consistent total error. It is dependent on the amount the mast twists, the exact position of the masthead unit – and the sails you put up will have an influence.

On some boats the errors will combine to make the apparent wind angle smaller than it should be, on others it will be bigger. Whichever way it goes, the error will be carried through into the calculation of the true wind angle. Not that you will tend to notice it here – whether or not the true wind angle is accurate to within 5 or 10 degrees will not be visible when you are using it for trimming or steering.

It is when the instruments use it to calculate the **true wind direction** that you will notice the problem. The true wind directon is worked out by adding the true wind angle to the heading (or course) if you are on starboard tack, and subtracting it if you are on port. Obviously if the true wind angle is wider or narrower than it should be, then the true wind direction will calculate to a different number on each tack:

- If the true wind angle is too **narrow**, then the true wind direction will be too far left on starboard tack compared to port
- If the true wind angle is too **wide** then the true wind direction will be too far right on starboard tack compared to port

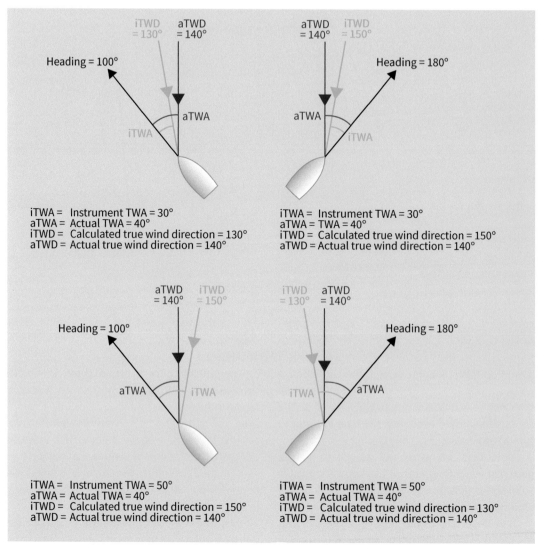

iTWA = Instrument TWA = 30°
aTWA = Actual TWA = 40°
iTWD = Calculated true wind direction = 130°
aTWD = Actual true wind direction = 140°

iTWA = Instrument TWA = 30°
aTWA = TWA = 40°
iTWD = Calculated true wind direction = 150°
aTWD = Actual true wind direction = 140°

iTWA = Instrument TWA = 50°
aTWA = Actual TWA = 40°
iTWD = Calculated true wind direction = 150°
aTWD = Actual true wind direction = 140°

iTWA = Instrument TWA = 50°
aTWA = Actual TWA = 40°
iTWD = Calculated true wind direction = 130°
aTWD = Actual true wind direction = 140°

Calibration of the true wind direction upwind

A secondary problem exists in that the amount of error in the true wind angle, be it wider or narrower, is not the same upwind to downwind. If you bear away from sailing upwind to reaching, on the same tack, you will find that the true wind direction changes even though the wind is steady.

We can conclude, firstly, that the true wind angle requires a correction at every point of sailing to make it read an accurate value. We need to develop a table of these corrections, for sailing upwind, reaching and downwind, at a band of wind speeds. Secondly, the way to develop the table is to use the errors we see in the true wind direction as we manoeuvre the boat, to tell us the corrections we need to make to the true wind angle.

We start by sailing upwind, preferably on a day when the breeze is not too shifty, making a note of the true wind speed and angle, and the true wind direction. The boat is then tacked, and after the instruments have settled (see the section on Damping – page 57) the new true wind direction is recorded. Take a note of the true wind angle and speed, and then tack back again, and see if the true wind goes back to where it was before. You want to be sure that the wind has not shifted while you were tacking, and any difference (or lack of it) in the true wind is genuine instrument error and not a wind shift.

Once you are satisfied, work out the correction to the true wind angle required. If the true wind direction on port tack is further right than it is on starboard, i.e. 150° on port compared to 130° on starboard, then the true wind angle is too narrow. (It is too wide if the true wind direction on starboard is further right compared to that on port.)

The amount of the correction is found by dividing the difference between the two true winds by two, and in the case where the true wind angle is too narrow, adding it on. So in this case we would add:

$$(150° – 130°) ÷ 2 = 10°$$

to the true wind angle to correct it.

Once you are confident of the correction required upwind, try sailing along close-hauled and then bearing away to a close reach, perhaps at a 60° true wind angle. Again you should watch the true wind direction for any changes, and repeat the exercise several times to be sure that the changes are due to the instruments and not the wind.

Let's take an example – sailing along upwind on port tack and the true wind direction reads 200°. Then when you bear away to 60° true wind angle, the true wind direction changes to 210°. To calibrate this error, we know that we must add the whole of the difference between the two true winds, which is 10°, as a correction to the true wind angle at 60°.

Another example, we are now on starboard tack sailing at 120° true wind angle. The wind speed is steady and the true wind direction is 300° after it has been corrected upwind. We bear away to 160° true wind angle and the true wind alters to 315°. What is the correction required for the 160° true wind angle?

The correction is 15°, the difference between the two true wind directions. Now we just need to work out whether it should be added or taken away from the 160° true wind angle. Because we are on starboard and the true wind direction goes right, this means that the true wind angle is being calculated too wide. So we should subtract the 15° to calibrate out the error. Another way of thinking about it is to work out what you need to do to the true wind angle to change 315° to 300°, and the answer must be, for starboard tack, to subtract 15°.

Eventually, you must slowly and repeatedly manoeuvre the boat through the full range of sailing angles, carefully calculating the necessary corrections to keep the true wind direction the same.

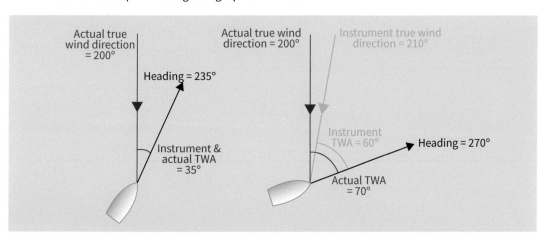

Calibration of the true wind direction on a reach

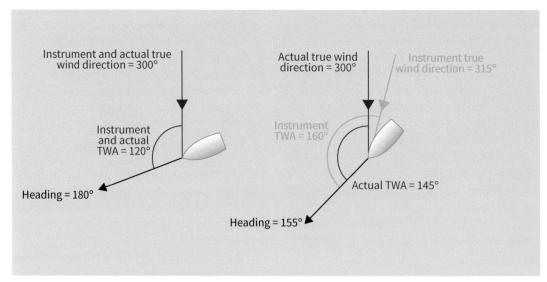

Calibration of the true wind direction downwind

So what do we do with our table of corrections once we have worked it out? These days many instrument systems have built-in tables that allow you to enter the corrections, a system that was first developed by Mark and used on the Sailmath Deckman in the late 1980s. It has subsequently been adopted by many other instrument systems. The instruments can automatically apply the corrections depending on the wind speed and angle you are sailing at. Alternatively, if the instrument system doesn't have this facility, if the boat has a computer and navigation software, then it's often possible to put the table in there.

Completing this calibration process accurately is critical to effective use of the boat's instrument system and other electronics. Take the situation where you are coming into a port-rounding leeward mark, right behind another boat that you are catching fast (diagram below). You need to know whether you want to start the next beat on port or starboard so you can choose which side to overtake him on.

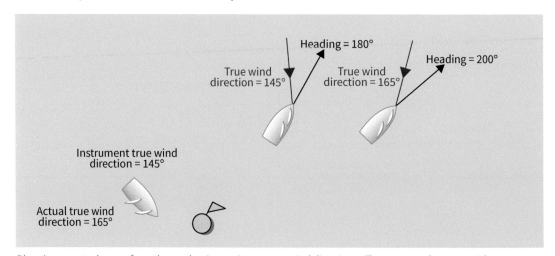

Planning your tack away from the mark using an inaccurate wind direction will put you on the wrong side

You need to know the wind direction on the boat before rounding the leeward mark

Let's assume there is no TWA calibration table. Not unnaturally you look at your true wind direction to see which tack is favoured, and it says the wind direction is 145°. From your wind readings up the last beat you know that this is a big port tack lift. In which case you would be happy to go round outside him at the mark, so long as you can get clear air, rather than push for an inside overlap.

So you decide to go to leeward of him. As soon as you round the mark and set up upwind, the TWD reading you see is now 165°. Fail. This is not the left shift you thought. The other boat is pinning you on port and until you can clear him you are stuck in the header – no way to start a new beat ...

If the boat has the correct correction table it will automatically subtract those 20° from the true wind angle downwind, to get the same true wind direction that you had upwind. So you subtract 20° from the true wind angle on port and this moves the true wind direction right to 165°. It puts rather a different complexion on things knowing this before the mark. You promptly slow the boat down and round the mark neatly behind the other boat. Now you can tack immediately after the mark and get on that lifted starboard tack.

One final comment, and this is the bad news, there is absolutely no guarantee that once you have worked out your true wind angle correction table that it will work for more than a few minutes ...!

A howl of anguish would be appropriate here ... understandably aghast that so much work can be so easily destroyed. Experience has taught us that the conditions of wind sheer and gradient have an effect on the calibration corrections required. The exact mechanics are complex, but it's easy to imagine how a much lighter breeze at water level might be deflected more than a stronger one – and so you need more or less correction for the same wind speed value at the masthead. There are also secondary effects: for instance, the changes in wind gradient and sheer will impact the mast twist, as the mainsail leech tension is altered and trimmed differently.

The only consolation is that, given typical conditions at a particular venue, the corrections seem to remain about the same, and when changes do occur they seem to be in the size of the correction rather than its direction. So once you have got your table for all the sailing angles it should work most days. However, doing a few tacks before the start to check it out is definitely recommended. And if the weather is unusual or you are sailing at a different venue (e.g. the Mediterranean rather than the Solent), then expect some very different numbers.

Wind sheer has a more obvious effect on the accuracy of the true wind direction. It rotates the numbers by however many degrees of sheer there is. So if you have 20° of wind sheer, which you can see from the difference in the apparent wind angle readings, then the wind you are sailing in is up to 20° different to the true wind direction you are reading on the dial.

A good way to check this is to work out what the wind should be from your headings on both tacks. If you are sailing at 200° on port tack and 270° on starboard tack then the wind should be blowing from 235° – halfway between the two headings. If the true wind dial reads 245° then you have ten degrees of wind sheer.

Another way of checking before the start is to go head to wind with the boom flapping on the centreline and see if the compass heading is the same as the true wind direction.

The main reason you need to watch out for wind sheer errors is for laylines and next leg calculations, which we will discuss in Chapter 5. But it is fairly evident that if you are using a wind direction that is 20° different from the one you are sailing in, it will throw out any calculations done by you or the navigation software for the next leg. At least it is an easy problem to deal with, just subtract the right number of degrees until the wind sheer goes away.

It's worth checking to see if the instrument system or navigation software provides the facility to correct wind sheer separately to the apparent wind angle calibration. This is a useful facility, allowing you to correct sheer without losing track of the base calibration.

Don't Panic!!

Sometimes, despite all your effort, the instruments seem out of kilter with reality.

> MARK: It's a long time ago, but the most extreme and difficult conditions I ever faced were in Kiel Week way back in 1989. It was the British trials for the Admiral's Cup team and the first real racing for a very carefully set up instrument and computer system aboard the IOR fifty-footer, *Jamarella*. It was halfway through one of the inshore races, and, according to the instruments, we were sailing straight into the wind, with an apparent wind angle of zero degrees and a breeze of ten knots. Meanwhile the sails were full and the water was a glassy calm.

Confused? Don't be – although this is a very extreme example, such apparent instrument anomalies are relatively commonplace. The crew's response is just as common, "There's something wrong with the instruments." It's a phrase that has a special place in every navigator's worst nightmares. But in this instance there was nothing wrong with the equipment. It was still telling us something useful, but the message needed more interpretation. Producing good information when you cannot read the number directly off the dial is one of the key skills of the navigator. So what was going on that day in Kiel?

It was wind sheer and wind gradient. There was little or no mixing of the wind aloft and down on the water, so there were big differences in wind speed. It is perfectly possible that the wind 80 feet up is travelling at ten knots whilst at zero feet it is stationary – and that's what the instruments were telling us. The masthead unit can only measure the wind speed where it is.

This information can be of use to the trimmers, they need a very different trim at the bottom to the top, and it has to take account of both the difference in speed and in direction. We were able

to fill the sails on *Jamarella* even though the wind at the masthead was coming from dead ahead, because the wind halfway down the mast was blowing from further to the left (we were on port tack) and filling the sails.

Again the instruments were telling us all they knew, and the information was certainly of interest to the trimmers. It just needed interpreting correctly. So the next time the trimmer says, "There's something wrong with the instruments." Don't panic! Not only are they quite possibly wrong, but they are the people who need the real information the most.

Damping: High Or Low?

Most instrument systems provide some facility for damping the data that they produce. The damping (or filtering, to use the more technical name) does just what the name suggests – controls the speed of response of the numbers you see on the dial to changes in the raw data.

The maths of damping can be done in lots of different ways, but the simplest is to average the data coming from the sensors over a variable period of time. The shorter the period of time, the quicker the values on the dial will respond to changes. This can be advantageous for seeing changes quickly, but you may well find that the numbers jump around so much that it is impossible to tell what they mean. In this case you need a longer damping period to average out all the small, quick changes so that you get a clearer view of the overall picture.

Usually there is a happy medium between quick response and smooth changes, but it will be different for different conditions. In big breezes and waves the boat, and therefore the instruments, will be jumping around a lot more and so the numbers will need more damping. In light airs and flat water, you can bring the damping right down so that you can pick up the changes in those zephyrs really fast.

The time it takes for the true wind direction to settle on its new value after a tack is one of the biggest bugbears for the tactician. There are a couple of things going on here. One is that the flow of the wind over the sails and the water over the keel takes time to get established and stabilise on the new tack. This is an inevitable part of the physics of fluid flow, it works itself out slowly as the boat accelerates, and can take up to a minute to disappear completely.

The second problem is that the damping (and performance, as described in Mark's anecdote) of the sensors means that they respond to the change in direction in the manoeuvre at different rates. The wind angle will respond much more quickly than the compass for instance. And until they have settled on an accurate value, the wrong number will be going into the wind angle and wind direction calculations. This results in an inaccurate spike that's most visible in the true wind direction during a tack, gybe, round up or bear away. It can easily take thirty seconds after a tack is completed

MARK: The idea of using a 'look-up' table to calibrate the true wind angle slowly spread to become a widespread feature of modern instrument systems and navigation software. It solved the problem of what we can call 'static' errors in the wind direction – the wind could now be calibrated accurately when sailing steadily in a straight line.

Once that problem was solved it revealed another that occurred during manoeuvres. We can call these 'dynamic' errors in the true wind direction. They were created when the boat tacked, gybed or rounded a mark. Initially I dealt with this just by ignoring the 'spike' in the wind direction. We know from wind tunnels and CFD that it takes time for the flow of wind over the sails to re-establish after a manoeuvre anyway, and I put the spike down to this effect.

I slowly became convinced that this wasn't the only thing going on. It was during the 2003 America's Cup (when sailing with One World) that I had the motivation and resources to get to the bottom of the problem, because the pre-start manoeuvres were making the wind direction completely unusable, right at the time when we needed it most.

It took a while, but I eventually realised the spike was coming from lags in the input data to the wind direction calculation. We were using a fluxgate compass and they have a significant lag in the measurement of heading when the boat is turning. In comparison, the apparent wind angle sensor has almost no lag in its measurement. So during a turn, the heading data going into the wind direction calculation was a couple of seconds behind where the boat was actually pointing, while the apparent wind angle was up to date with the movement. This led to an error, or spike, in the true wind direction that would slowly disappear in time as the fluxgate compass caught up.

It was a couple more years before I could test the theory, when working with Peter Harrison's short-lived challenge for the 2007 America's Cup. Mark Sheffield had got hold of an early version of what we'd now call a MEMs or Fibre Optic Gyro that provided much, much more responsive heading data. I still remember the first time we went out to test it, after we'd got it connected to the instrument system. We bore away quickly after a head to wind mainsail hoist, and the true wind direction stayed steady as a rock.

The price, size and weight of these devices has come down greatly over the intervening years, and if you can afford them, they are definitely a great addition to the boat's instrument armoury.

for the true wind direction to find its new value.

It is really important to remember this; reading it too soon will lead to problems whether you are calibrating, wind tracking before the start or on the racecourse. A lot will depend on the quality of the sensors you have on board – a really good heading sensor will make a big difference and provide much smoother wind direction data.

Some advanced systems allow for what is called 'dynamic damping'. This allows the navigator to use a different damping when the boat is on a steady course, compared to when it is tacking or gybing. Overall, we can say that damping is a key element that the navigator has to adjust to make sure the trimmers, tactician and helmsman make the most out of the data.

Advanced Calibration & Wrap Up

Generally speaking, the more advanced the system, the more freedom the user has to create tables and coefficients, or even mathematical functions to calibrate the numbers.

For instance, an advanced instrument system or navigation software will make it possible to have tables for a boat speed correction based on heel. This means that the dependence of the boat speed measurement on heel can be corrected (due to differing water flow around the boat speed sensor). It's also possible to create different true wind speed correction tables for different sails (as we mentioned earlier), or leeway tables for different configurations, and much more.

The overall concept and key takeaway is that the physics of sailing is complex and there are many different elements that influence the numbers produced. Follow the steps highlighted in this chapter but always be ready to challenge your own work and be open to realising that the conditions have changed. It is very difficult to have a perfectly calibrated system, but a very good way to understand how far you are from it, is to look at the true wind direction and the current (or

tidal) data that the system is calculating. These calculations use multiple other variables, and if things are not working properly then you will notice asymmetry or strange behaviour in those numbers.

Navigation software plays a key role in helping you understand this and optimising your calibration, but we will see this in the analysis section.

Load Cells

In highly competitive boats and systems, there can be many more pieces in the calibration puzzle both from the sensors' side and from the processor and software side than the ones we have seen so far.

Looking at the sensors, more and more boats are installing load sensors and pressure sensors for hydraulic systems, or position sensors for deflectors or other mechanical parts.

The calibration of these is usually done with offsets tables and / or by comparing with a reference measure. Each sensor has its own specification and reading the manual and discussing with the supplier is the best way forward. The good news is that these numbers don't affect the wind calculation (but they affect performance and data analysis, so should be well calibrated anyway!).

Looking at the processor and software, generally speaking the rule that applies is 'the more advanced the system, the more freedom the user has to create tables and coefficients, or even mathematical functions to calibrate the numbers'.

For instance, an advanced instrument system or navigation software will make it possible to have tables for a boat speed correction based on heel. This means that the dependence of the boat speed measurement on heel can be corrected (due to differing water flow around the boat speed sensor).

It's also possible to create different true wind speed correction tables for different sails (as we mentioned earlier), or leeway tables for different configurations, and much more …

59

In the previous chapters, we have discussed how to get accurate instrument data. In this chapter, we will discuss how to look at the numbers during the race, and make sure everyone on board gets the most out of the information available.

Our general approach in writing this chapter has been to look at the problem from the perspective of racecourse geometry and analysis, and then understand how this can be done with navigation software. This approach allows us to understand the data and get much more confident with it, and it especially helps to understand possible weak links in the information that everyone should be aware of.

Start Lines & Wind Shifts

The start of the race will be the first test for your instrument system. The navigator will have two main jobs to do:

- Work out which end of the line has the advantage
- Understand the best tack off the start

For both of these tasks you will need to use the true wind direction. We will leave aside such concerns as general strategy for the course, be it tidal or wind, and any impact this might have on the end of the line or the first tack.

Choosing which **end of the line** to start from means choosing the one closest to the wind. To work this out we first need to calculate what we are going to call the 'neutral line wind'. This is the true wind direction that is completely square to the line. The easiest way to work it out is to take a bearing along the line, then add 90° if you took the bearing from the starboard end or subtract 90° if the bearing is from the port end. The result of this calculation is the neutral line wind, or the true wind direction for which there is no bias, no advantage to starting at one end or the other. If the wind moves right from this neutral line wind then the starboard end will be favoured, and if it moves left then port end is favoured. So once you know the neutral line wind direction, all it then takes is a glance at the true wind direction to tell you the favoured end.

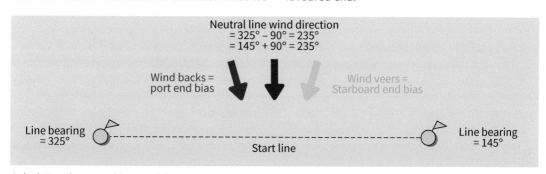

Neutral line wind direction
= 325° − 90° = 235°
= 145° + 90° = 235°

Wind backs = port end bias

Wind veers = Starboard end bias

Line bearing = 325°

Line bearing = 145°

Start line

Calculating the neutral line wind direction

If the boat is equipped with navigation software, then you can ping the end of the lines (i.e. you insert the coordinates of both ends of the line into the app) and the software will do all the maths for you and tell you the three most important pieces of data:

- Which end is favoured
- How much bias there is in terms of metres / boat lengths (the longer the line, the more advantage in terms of boat lengths you get from starting on the correct side)
- The neutral line wind direction

There are now two things to consider:

- The wind direction is not always stable
- In the pre-start, there may well be a lot of boats manoeuvring, including your own, and this will generate a lot of turbulence in the wind

Let's discuss one of these at a time. By monitoring the wind direction in the 30 minutes or so before the start you should be able to see if there are some trends. If the wind is oscillating, you may need to anticipate the shift that you will be on at start time.

Imagine a situation where at nine minutes to go the port end is biased, but by six minutes to go the wind has swung and the starboard end now gets the nod. With three minutes to go it is back to the port end – but if you made the decision to head that way you might well find that at the start gun the starboard end is favoured.

Tracking these shifts down to start time can be done by writing the time and number on the display or (more easily if you have it) looking at the time graphs in the navigation software. But we must keep in mind all that we have said in the previous sections about calibration and damping. It's important to check the calibration of the true wind before you start taking wind readings. Calibration errors are often particularly severe when the boat is tacking from reach to reach – which tends to happen quite a lot before the start.

Don't be fooled into thinking that there are huge wind shifts around when there are not. Damping is another problem when the boat is being thrown

GILBERTO: Palma is known as a great sailing venue. Great conditions with a sea breeze are typical in the bay and both Olympic classes and keelboats have great events there. But, even so, there are days where conditions are very unstable with storms on the island and at sea affecting the conditions quite significantly.

I remember one spring race there with these cloudy / rainy conditions. The start was set and the countdown was on. Apparently all was going well with a typical starboard approach with my boat aiming at the middle of the line. We had a good spot, free from other boats, with 20 seconds to burn and 1 minute to go. Suddenly, I felt the boat losing pressure. I looked up and quickly realised that the whole fleet was 'de-powered'; the wind was being sucked by a big cloud next to the racecourse. By the time I looked back down at the tablet again the scenario and numbers had changed. There was nothing to burn and we could actually come up all the way to the committee quarter of the line. I called 'full racing' and pushed the tactician to go up 20°. We had a great start.

I was lucky enough to have a good system on board and to be in a position where I trusted the numbers (no dirty air around me) and was fast enough to understand the situation. Some other boats where a lot slower in realising the big change and came late to the start. In those moments, having a clear picture of how much to trust the numbers you are seeing is key.

around in the starting area; particularly when it is combined with lots of dirty wind from all the sails and confused seas. In fact, when it comes down to it, you will be hard pushed to get a decent reading when you get into the final approach to the line. To mitigate this effect you can freeze the true wind direction in the navigation software. This has all the pros and cons that you can imagine: on one side you will have very steady numbers, on the other you might miss a shift just before the start.

The start line requires the navigator to multi-task

The start is a time when you must try to multi-task across whatever your role is for the start itself (perhaps calling time to the line or time to burn if this isn't on a display) and think ahead to the first couple of minutes of the beat.

Your first job is to work out what the wind is doing as you come off the line. So, you have to know whether the instruments are settled on the number they are showing, or just spinning past it as the damping tries to cope with some radical manoeuvre the boat has just executed. In short, you need to watch it all the time. It is never easy to ignore the excitement of a start, but you look pretty average when, as soon as you are off the line, the tactician turns round and asks, "Are we up or down?" and you do not know.

One complication you need not worry about is the effect of the tide on the start line wind.

Sometimes an inexperienced race officer will set a badly biased line. The reason for this is that he is measuring the wind direction from a boat that is anchored to the seabed – and so it is the ground wind that he is recording. If the boat is sailing in water that is moving relative to the seabed, then the true wind will have a tide wind component, as we mentioned in the section on the wind triangle (page 35).

This tide wind component can alter the wind you are sailing in quite dramatically. So, if you ignore the tide and set the line to the ground wind, you may well have a substantial bias. The good news is that your onboard instruments (assuming that you are not also anchored) will read the true wind that includes the tidal component. It is only the race officer, who is anchored, that must account for it in his calculations (see overleaf).

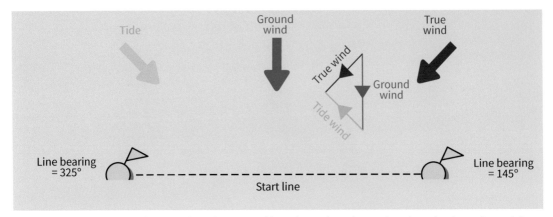

The line would be square to the ground wind, measured from the anchored committee boat, but has substantial starboard bias to the tidally-altered true wind

One final point about wind shift tracking. We mentioned earlier that changes in wind gradient and sheer may affect the calibration of the true wind direction. This poses a problem; how are you supposed to recognise calibration that has altered whilst you are racing?

If, for instance, it started altering when you tacked, in a manner that your calibration did not account for, how would you know? Would you not just assume that the wind was shifting as you tacked? For a while you might, but after this happens three or four times you ought to be suspicious. But three or four tacks on dud information could cost you the race, so here is a check that you can use. Keep a note of your compass headings on each tack as a back-up. These will also tell you if you are headed or lifted, so as soon as you are worried that the true wind direction is playing up you can check what it is telling you against the heading.

Unfortunately, there is a problem with this as well, since the true wind angle that many yachts sail at is dependent on the wind strength. The stronger the wind, the closer you can sail to the wind, until about fifteen or twenty knots when the angle does not get any narrower and may even widen as the wind increases towards thirty knots.

So, based solely on the compass data, it might look like a header or a lift, but only the wind speed has altered, and not the wind direction. This is known as a velocity header or lift. It is accentuated by what happens to your apparent wind when the true wind first changes. The diagram opposite shows the case of a velocity header.

As the wind drops, the boat has sufficient momentum to keep its speed for a few seconds, which moves the apparent wind forward, backs the jib and gives the impression that you have been headed. It is important that the helmsman does not bear away too hard when this happens because, as the boat slows down to match the new wind speed, the jib will stop backing, and you can gain ground to windward by holding course and letting the speed drop until the jib refills. You will have to bear away a little because of the new wider true wind angle for the lower wind speed.

If you have confidence in the true wind direction then you will see this for what it is – a change in wind speed, rather than a change in wind direction. So don't be fooled into tacking by the velocity header. It's just as important to be careful when checking the true wind direction against the compass heading that you do not start worrying about the true wind direction unnecessarily. The true wind will ignore velocity headers and lifts, whereas the compass will not. So you really have to keep an eye on them both, each to check the other. In the next section we will see how we can use the heel angle to help with a similar problem with the true wind speed.

1. Initial situation

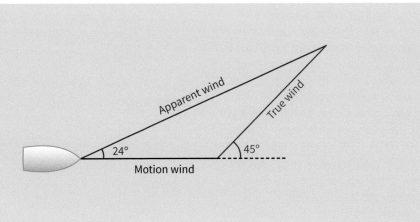

2. The wind drops, but boat speed maintains

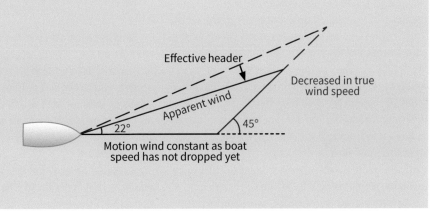

3. Boat slows down

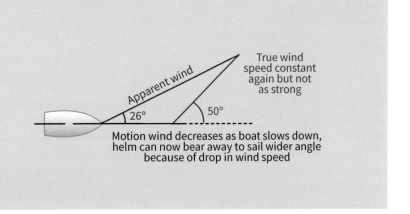

The velocity header

Heel Angle Or Wind Speed?

We previously cited an example, albeit extreme, where the wind speed read ten knots at the top of the mast, and the water was a glassy calm. The effect of wind sheer and gradient meant the instruments required careful interpretation. We looked at how to deal with the apparent wind angle, but not the wind speed, which you need for sail selection and target speeds.

So what do you do when the wind is seriously mixed up about how windy it is? The answer is to use the heel angle.

At any sailing angle other than downwind the heel can be an excellent

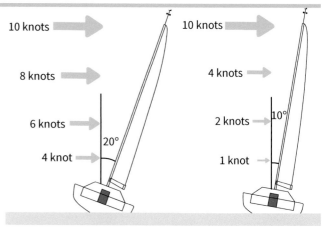

The effect of wind gradient on heel angle

measure of how much power there is in the wind. This is what you are using the wind speed to tell you, so that you can match your sails to the wind available. Under average conditions of wind gradient, the wind speed is a reasonably good guide. But it will always be limited by the fact that it is only measuring the wind speed in one place. And the wind can and will change at a height other than the masthead. In this case, the only way the instruments will pick up the change in the force available from the wind is via the heel angle.

Before we go any further, we should put in a proviso about the heel angle not just being dependent on the wind speed; sail choice, trim, steering technique, etc. will all effect it as well. But when you are sailing along in a straight line and all these things are more or less constant, and suddenly the heel angle starts dropping – while the wind speed remains the same – it should be clear

what is happening.

This type of thing is most often seen in the Mediterranean, which is prone to the light and fickle conditions where this technique is useful. It's a place where the wind sheer comes and goes, or bands of warmer air blow in which are less dense and therefore exert less force or pressure. This is when wind speed measurement becomes less than trustworthy.

Keeping an eye on the heel angle can give you that vital first clue to what is going on. But do not expect the technique to work when you are crashing upwind in twenty knots: the heel angle will be jumping around far too much to be useful, unless your instrument system has the facility to damp it. Fortunately, in these conditions the wind is usually steady and consistent at all heights and the wind speed does the job it was intended for perfectly well.

Anticipation

In the second chapter we made the point that anticipation is not so much an instrument technique as a vital state of mind for the navigator. Because of the greater emphasis on tactics in short course racing, you will spend less time working on strategy and more supporting the tactician with the information he or she needs for his or her decisions.

The key to doing the navigator's job well is to anticipate what the tactician is going to want to know next and start working it out before he asks for it. There are endless possible examples, and we have pointed out a couple below. But if there was one single piece of advice we would give to a big boat navigator on this subject, it is to do some small boat racing as a helmsman and decision maker. There is no faster way to get an insight into what the tactician needs to know. Then read all the books on yacht racing tactics as well as those on navigating.

The first example comes up all the time. You are on port tack heading towards the starboard tack layline, and apparently on a collision course with two yachts on starboard tack. The tactician needs to know whether or not those boats are laying the mark before you get to them. He has to decide whether to duck behind them or tack underneath. If they are laying the mark comfortably then a tack to leeward and slightly ahead will see you round in front. If they are not laying, it would be preferable for you to duck behind them and sail on to the layline. The navigator should see this coming way before it arrives, particularly in a tidal situation where it is much harder to judge the layline by eye.

We are going back into ancient history for the second example, with another anecdote from Mark (see opposite).

The wind shift coming through when it did made the move look particularly smart – but starting to look at the question before it was asked was the only way to have the answer ready in time. A good tactician will expect this sort of anticipation; it is not his job to be warning you of every possible situation that might arise. He is going to ask the question when he needs the answer, which is usually immediately. So keep your eyes on the racecourse, concentrate and anticipate.

Fortunately, the navigation software is designed to help the navigator to speed up the process of calculating scenarios and thinking about geometry, the next leg and more. As we mentioned earlier, one of the great features of navigation software is the ability to do 'What If?' calculations.

This can be used in multiple ways. Imagine that you notice that the wind has started to go left constantly, and in the last 10 minutes it has shifted by 6°. You are still 15 minutes away from the mark. What will the next leg look like? What if the wind goes back right? What if it continues to go left? You can quickly do the maths in the software and picture the scenarios in your head, before you get asked. Many of the 'What If?' scenarios involve geometry and times closely related to the boat's polar tables. We will next look closely at instrument techniques that have polars as the key element. We have highlighted and separated the two sections clearly so that the reader has a very clear understanding that some parts of navigation with instruments can be done independently from the polars, but others are closely related and inaccurate polar curves will lead to mistakes.

MARK: I still remember the final inshore of the 1989 Admiral's Cup. A left shift had come in on the first beat and we were sailing to the gybe mark on a tight reach, fourth of the fifty-footers. The last of the leading three peeled round and gybed, when we were about fifty yards from the mark. The tactician asked if we could carry on, meaning had the wind swung enough to make the next leg a run rather than a reach? If it was a run we could start it on either gybe, but preferably the one that was most advantaged by the present wind shift. I had been looking at the problem for a minute or so: it was certainly a run; the question was whether or not starboard put us on the best shift. By the time the question came I was able to answer 'yes'. The gybe was cancelled, we squared away and carried on on starboard. A couple of minutes went by and the breeze lifted us, which downwind takes you away from the mark. So we gybed, and, now laying the mark on the paying tack, ran down to it and into second place.

CHAPTER 5

Instrument Techniques

Using The Polar Table

Before we dig deeper into instrument techniques using polar tables, we have to explain one rather confusing concept. Every boat will need more than one polar table if the navigation software is to be used effectively – this might seem puzzling at first, because we've said that the polar table defines the optimum performance of the boat, but we can explain ...

We have seen throughout the book that polar tables are difficult to calculate, and that the wind conditions each day can be very different, even if the readings for true wind speed at the top of the mast are the same.

For example, on two different days the wind sensor reads the true wind speed as 10kts, but on the first day the boat sails at its polar table targets of 7kts boat speed and 45° true wind angle, while on the second day it exceeds them with 7.3kts at 42° true wind angle. So how should we handle this difference?

On the one hand, from a performance analysis perspective (we will discuss this more in the next chapter), you shouldn't adjust your targets day by day. On the other hand, we can't expect the navigation software to be accurate for laylines and timings on the second day, when we are sailing at a different angle and speed to the polar table in the navigation software.

The way this problem is tackled is by having at least two polar tables in the software. One is the performance polar; a fixed target for the season and displayed as the target for the trimmers and helmsman. The second is usually called the navigation polar and is adjusted day by day. This is the one that the software uses to calculate all the values that are useful for navigation like the laylines, next leg times and so on.

There is often a third set of polars which are used for the starting procedure. Again, these polars are slightly different from the other ones, as during the start you might be happy to pinch slightly higher than usual VMG angles, and the boat will struggle to reach full speed as the wind is dirty and turbulent. So, from now on, we will discuss techniques referring to the different polars that we have mentioned above.

Start Procedure

We have already discussed all the problems and issues of wind shifts and bias on the start line, and encouraged navigators to look ahead to the first leg – but what else is the navigator asked to do during the start?

The 'magical number' that the navigator is giving to the team (and especially to the tactician) is the time to burn. This number tells the crew if the boat is early or late to the start, and by how much. How is this calculated by the navigation software and what should the navigator worry about to make it more accurate and reliable?

The inputs that go into the calculation are:
• Wind speed
• Boat speed

- Position of the boat
- Position of the start line
- Starting polars
- Acceleration table
- Rate of turn table

Basically, to understand how fast a boat can go from the current position to having the bow on the start line, the system needs to know all these things. And a single error in one of them will lead to a misleading burn time number.

We have seen how to make most of those inputs as accurate as possible. What we have not seen before is the acceleration table and the rate of turn table.

These two tables are designed to tell the software how fast a boat is accelerating in certain conditions (in particular, with a specific wind speed and a specific true wind angle), and how quickly the boat can turn (in degrees per second) in the same conditions.

If you are sailing parallel to the line with flapping sails, the software is doing the following maths:

- Calculating how long it takes to accelerate the boat from this speed to the target speed, while turning the boat from this true wind angle to the optimum VMG angle (assuming an upwind or downwind start), otherwise to the true wind angle to the first mark
- Calculating how long it takes for the boat to cover the remaining distance to the line (once the first condition has been achieved), at the optimum VMG angle and target starting polar speed

Sum up the numbers, and you will have how much time the software thinks it will take you to reach the start line. Subtract this time from the time remaining to the start, and you will get the burn time, or time to burn.

If we want to see the formula, we can represent it like this:

Burn Time =

(Countdown to start) – (Time to reach the line)

Of course, the time to reach the line changes if you consider doing a gybe or a tack, etc.

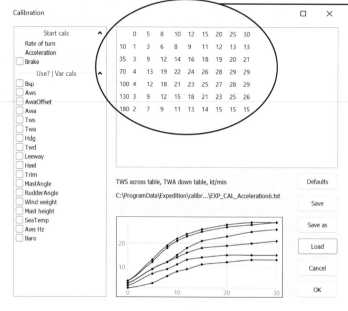

This table represents the acceleration of the boat (in kts per min) in different conditions. The columns show TWS (0 to 30 in kts), and the rows show TWA (10° to 180°).

For example, in 12kts of wind speed and at 70° TWA, we expect the boat to accelerate at a rate of 24kts per min – this doesn't mean it will go from dead in the water to 24kts in 1min. It means that if it was blowing at 12kts, the boat was sailing at 70° TWA and had 4kts of boat speed, then it would take it another 20 seconds to get to its top speed (or polar speed) in those conditions of 12kts. (12kts – 4kts = 8 kts; 8kts ÷ 24kts = 1/3; 1/3 x 1min = 20sec)

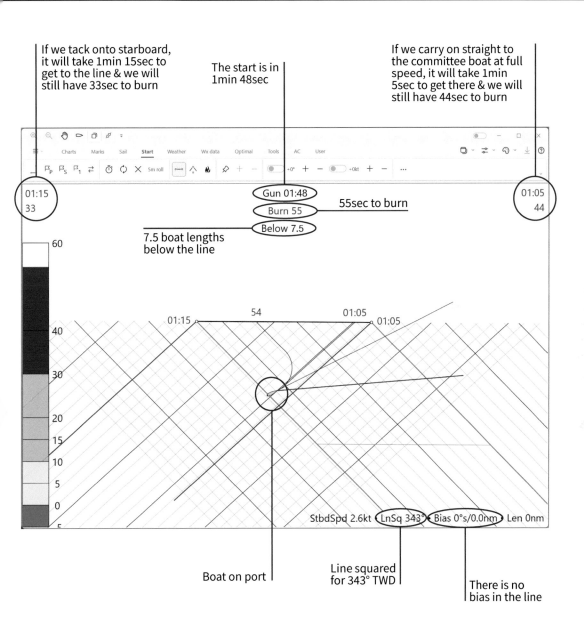

A screenshot of the pre-start view on Expedition showing the geometry of the line and timings for different approaches

So, it should be clear by now that to get the right time to burn requires a lot of accurate calculation and a lot of work making the inputs to that calculation accurate. It is very important that the navigator understands this and does a bit of extra work in his mind taking into consideration what he sees around him, for example:

- The wind is very dirty because you are in a busy spot on the start, so think that the boat will accelerate slower than what the computer is calculating
- The sea state is a bit more choppy than the usual conditions for that wind speed, so think that the boat will struggle to get up to speed

- There are some puffs coming, so be careful because the boat will accelerate faster than expected and you might find yourself on the line early

Overall, all of these considerations are standard for a tactician. What we want to highlight is that the navigator can't look at the numbers and rely on them a hundred percent. Part of the role is to interpret those numbers and understand when you can read them as they are, and when you have to tweak them in your head. Especially at the start.

Knowing the burn time is essential for a good start

Laylines

The theory behind laylines is very simple. If you have your polars, you know the target true wind angle that optimises the velocity made good. Whenever the boat is at the point where the course between the boat and the mark requires sailing at that wind angle to the wind direction, then you can tack, and that will optimise your time to the mark. The imaginary line that connects all the points where you can tack is called the layline. If you are sailing without navigation software, then this must be calculated by eye or with a hand-bearing compass.

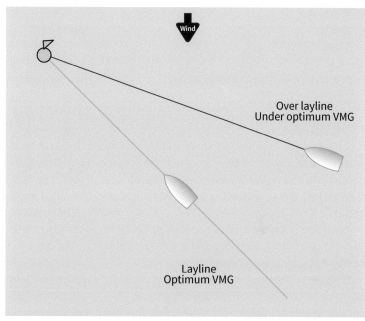

One boat on the layline and the other not

As easy as it sounds, getting the laylines right is one of the key tasks for the navigator and the reason why boats started to have computers and software on board.

Hitting the laylines is a key task for the navigator

There are three main obstacles between a navigator and a perfect layline:

- Current
- Polars
- Wind shifts

Let's discuss them one at the time.

Current

As we discussed in the calibration section, current is at the end of all the calculations that the system makes and so any errors are often amplified in this number. As the layline calculation is affected by the current, this is something we have to worry about.

Navigation software also allows you to 'not use' current in the calculation, and this is a safe option if you are worried about its reliability.

Even when the current measurement is reliable, we have to consider that, on the racecourse, the current might change from the moment we tack to the moment we get to the mark. This can be due to the geometry of the course (consider a top mark set up close to a river exit, for example) or a tide change.

Polars

We have said many times in this book: every day on the water is different. The wind behaviour changes, and we have to adjust how we sail with it.

For the layline calculation, the navigation software should use the navigation polars, and these should be adjusted almost every day. When going out in the morning and doing warm up upwind and downwind sessions with tacks and gybes, the navigator should closely look at the true wind angles that the boat is sailing at. The layline calculations for the day will likely need to use those angles.

We expect these angles to change one or two degrees, not much more, but when you are calling long laylines or for very tight calls with the competition, they can make a difference. So make sure you always have an eye on the angles the boat is doing that particular day, and make sure the software factors that in.

GILBERTO: Porto Cervo is one of the best sailing venues in the world, but the laylines can be really hard. I remember one particular day sailing in the Swan Cup, and the race committee had set up a windward / leeward course with a top mark not far from the Isola delle Bisce. The north-westerly wind (typical Mistral) had been blowing strongly the previous few days, but this day started with a nice 15kt breeze that was slowly dropping.

On the first upwind we were doing quite well and free from the fleet, and I had time to decide with no tactical pressure where to tack for the layline. We were quite far from the mark and I chose a comfortable layline. For several minutes we were pointing straight at the mark and the boat was going fine. All of a sudden, we started to point lower and lower. The last minute to the mark was very painful and at the end we had to double tack.

What was going on? The wind on the water was looking stable, there was no land effect I could think of … I was puzzled.

On the second leg we were more in the middle of the fleet and started a tacking duel in the centre of the course, so I really didn't have the chance to test my layline skills again. Back at home, I reviewed the regatta on the navigation software and the wind and current data. And the answer becomes apparent. As we approached the top mark we entered an area of strong current coming out of the channel. Nothing changed on the ground wind, but the true wind was strongly affected by the current.

Wind Shifts

We all know that the wind can be very shifty, and every shift means that the laylines move. So, how do we use the instruments and the numbers that they give us to help us navigate with this complexity?

Let's consider a venue where the land is causing a constant shift on one side of the course. One useful feature of the software is to record your track over the ground during the race. If the first time you go to the layline you fall short (even if by eye it looks 'ok'), the second time you go to that side of the course you know that you can keep that track as a reference and go beyond it. Sometimes it can help you find a sweet spot where you get connected to a different wind; and having that in your system as a track or waypoint is a smart move.

The other option that the navigator has is to calculate or understand the time to the layline for different true wind directions. In this case, the instrument system or software might have a couple of features that are very useful. The first one is what's often called the layline true wind direction. This is a calculation of the true wind direction that would put you on the layline, right now, in your real-time position.

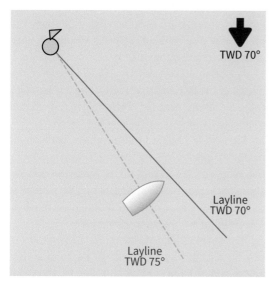

The software shows that the boat is on the layline if the wind goes to 75° TWD

The second feature is a function that we have already discussed called 'What If?'. This can help us calculate the distance and time to the layline if the wind shifts by 5° or 10°. A 'What If?' calculation in your navigation app allows the navigator to instantly see the changes that a wind shift will make to the current leg (or to calculate the tactical data required for smart decisions about the next leg, which we will come to next).

Without a 'What If?' calculation, you might get close to a corner and not even realise it. It can tell you how far you are from the layline at the extremes of the wind shift pattern. For instance, let's say that you are on port tack on a big lift, in fact, the wind is as far left as you have seen it with a true wind direction (TWD) of 80°, and the 'What If?' tells you that you have 5 minutes to go before you hit the starboard tack layline.

This is not the time to relax though – how far away is the starboard tack layline when a maximum right-hand shift (starboard tack lift) is a TWD of 120°? A 'What If?' calculation will tell you: it will recalculate all the sailing data based on this different wind direction. And now you might find that you are only a minute away from the starboard tack layline should the wind suddenly go back to the maximum right-hand shift – great information for a tactician trying to play the fleet up a busy beat.

A 'What If?' doesn't just help you make allowance for the wind shifts either, you can also use it to calculate the effect of more or less tide on the leg.

Let's say that you are beating up a shore, sticking tightly to the shallow water to duck a powerful current out in the channel. The software is calculating a current of maybe half a knot, and it says that the final starboard tack layline to the mark is ten minutes away.

Unfortunately, the mark is in the middle of the channel (isn't it always?) and you know that there is nearly four knots of current out there. So a layline calculated using half a knot of current is about as much use as an ashtray on a motorbike. The 'What If?' will allow you to enter the full value of the tide in the channel and it might then tell you that you have fifteen minutes until you reach that starboard tack layline.

We highly recommend that you carefully study the manual of your instrument system and navigation software to get the most out of its power to help understand and anticipate the changes to the geometry of the course that a wind shift brings.

Time To The Layline
When you are going upwind or downwind, tacking or gybing, it's essential to know how much time you have left on each tack. This is vital tactical information, not least because the general rule in a shifting breeze is to stay away from the corners of the racecourse. The 'time to the laylines' is probably the single most valuable piece of information the navigator can pass to the tactician, helmsman and the rest of the crew. It allows them to understand the geometry of the racecourse in

> **GILBERTO:** I remember jumping on board a boat a few years back to substitute another navigator just for one event. The tactician was very experienced and I was still quite young and green as navigator. We were sailing downwind to a gate; I started to give information about the layline times. In my head, it was clear that I was speaking about the left mark, as there had been a big shift in the wind and left was favoured by far.
>
> Indeed we ended up at the left mark, but at the end of the race the tactician looked at me and stated very clearly, "I need you to tell me always which mark you are referring to, don't forget."
>
> Lesson learnt. Whenever sailing downwind to a gate, it is very important for everyone to know if you are talking about one mark, the other or the middle of the gate. In some situations, you can just say "from now on, talking about left mark", in others, is better to repeat it when telling the times.

just two numbers.

These days I think most teams have settled on the same format for these two numbers. Always say the time to the layline directly ahead of the boat first, then the one on the opposite tack. And don't say anything extraneous, "three and two and a half" is all the tactician needs to know. When it's important, make eye contact first, and point ahead of you as you say the first number, then pause and point in the direction of the other tack or gybe as you say the second. There's much less chance for confusion or error.

Next Leg Calculations

Another key question for every sailor is: what will the next leg look like? In this case 'look like' of course refers to the wind angle that the boat will have to sail. The answer to this question affects the sail choice and other decisions the crew has to make.

The calculation you have to do is to find the range and bearing between the waypoint you are aiming at, and the next one. Then you can calculate the angle between the bearing and the true wind direction, and that angle is the next leg true wind angle. Fortunately this is another calculation that is done by the computer on board. This is one key piece of information that the crew often needs to prepare for a sail change, and this information has to be given early enough.

The other piece of information is related to the length of the leg, and that's how long it is going to take to sail the next leg. This is again calculated thanks to the polars we have in the system.

So, with the help of the computer, you should be able to quickly answer the question, *what about the next leg*? It's important to keep the answer short and clear – something like, "We have five minutes to the next mark, and then it's a reach at 100° TWA for around 15 to 20 minutes."

If you are sailing a coastal race, the next leg can be affected by the land; so be careful. The navigation software will not think to take you around a rock or a headland unless you tell it to do that.

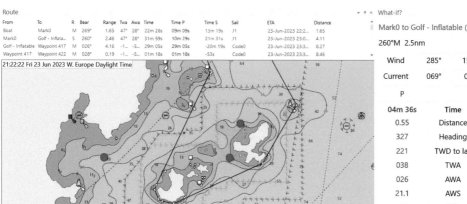

Route											
From	To	R	Bear	Range	Twa	Awa	Time	Time P	Time S	Sail	ETA	Distance
Boat	Mark0	M	269°	1.65	47°	28°	22m 28s	09m 09s	13m 19s	J1	23-Jun-2023 22:2...	1.65
Mark0	Golf - Inflata...	S	260°	2.46	47°	28°	31m 59s	10m 29s	21m 31s	J1	23-Jun-2023 23:0...	4.11
Golf - Inflatable	Waypoint 417	M	026°	4.16	-1...	-5...	29m 05s	29m 05s	-20m 19s	Code0	23-Jun-2023 23:3...	8.27
Waypoint 417	Waypoint 422	M	028°	0.19	-1...	-5...	01m 18s	01m 18s	-53s	Code0	23-Jun-2023 23:3...	8.46

21:22:22 Fri 23 Jun 2023 W. Europe Daylight Time

What-if?

Mark0 to Golf - Inflatable (S)

260°M 2.5nm   < >

Wind	285°	15.0kt	Held
Current	069°	0.5kt	Live

P		S
04m 36s	Time	19m 15s
0.55	Distance	2.29
327	Heading	247
221	TWD to lay	297
038	TWA	038
026	AWA	026
21.1	AWS	21.1
J2	Sail	J2

Expedition's tool for assessing the next leg. Looking at the table on the right-hand side, it is showing the leg from mark 0 to waypoint Golf (which is an inflatable to round to starboard). It is a bearing of 260° and a distance of 2.5nm. The wind data has been entered and the current data is coming live. On this basis, the bottom part of the table shows that this means 4min 36sec on port and 19min 15sec on starboard. This can help to plan, for example, the jib car set-up if you are coming from a reach

A technique to deal with this is to create 'sub-legs' with shorter and more accurate segments to go around an obstacle. So we might add to the information we gave initially by saying, "We have five minutes to the next mark, and then it's a reach at 100° TWA for around 15 to 20 minutes, but there is no room to go any lower as there are shallow rocks very close to the direct route. If the wind goes right by as little as 10°, we should be ready for a very quick sail change." This is a good numerical reference for the whole crew.

The 'What If?' calculation is also very useful in understanding the subtleties of the next leg tactics. Let's imagine that the next leg is a starboard tack reach and the tactician wants to know the true wind angle (TWA) that you will be sailing.

A 'What If?' calculation might say that it's a TWA of 130° – in the current TWD of 120°. If this is what you tell the

tactician, they might well be tempted to go for a spinnaker. But what if the maximum left-hand shift has been a TWD of 80°? A next leg 'What If?' calculation with a TWD of 80° will now say that the TWA will be 90° and the spinnaker is looking pretty extreme – a reaching sail would be the more conservative call.

Before the next leg, the crew need to know if the spinnaker is the best option

Velocity Made Good To The Course: VMC

The concept of velocity made good in the direction of the course (often shortened to VMC), is something you might have come across on your GPS. It is a simple enough idea, being the net velocity that you are making towards the mark, in the same way that VMG is the net velocity that you are making towards the wind. It is calculated in a similar fashion, being the velocity that you are making across the ground multiplied by the cosine of the angle between your COG and the course to the mark. As in the diagram, if X is the angle between your COG and the bearing of the mark then:

$$VMC = SOG \times Cosine \; X°$$

All these values are available to a GPS system which has a waypoint memory. Whether or not you should use it is another question altogether.

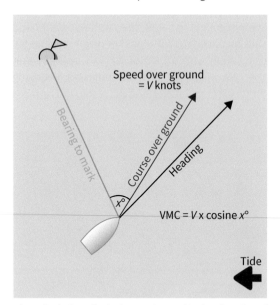

Speed over ground
= V knots

Bearing to mark

Course over ground

Heading

x°

VMC = V x cosine x°

Tide

The calculation of velocity made good in the direction of the course

VMC is a tactical and strategic tool that helps you follow the general rule, 'shorten the distance between you and the mark as quickly as possible'. It is most valuable when you have no idea what the weather or the current are likely to do.

If the geographical effects on the next leg are, to all intents and purposes, random, then your best strategy is usually to keep taking the option that gets you closest to the mark. Whatever the weather throws at you, you always have the least distance possible to sail – even if it is directly upwind!

The point to bear in mind is that there is almost always a faster way to sail the leg than by just optimising the VMC. The way to achieve this is to predict correctly the effects up the leg and then position the boat to make the best use of them. We will look at one approach to this shortly. But first there are a couple of points that we should make:
- Optimising your VMC on a reaching leg may not mean sailing straight at the mark
- Optimum VMC upwind is not necessarily the same as your optimum VMG

Taking the reaching leg case first, it may sound rather far-fetched to say that you can close on the mark faster by not sailing on the direct line towards it, but it all depends on the shape of the polar curve (see diagram).

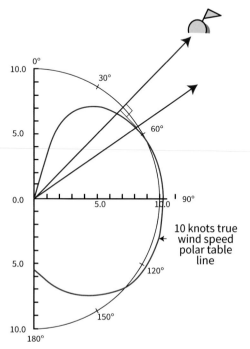

0°
10.0
30°
5.0
60°
0.0
5.0
10.0
90°
10 knots true
wind speed
polar table
line
5.0
120°
10.0
150°
180°

The optimum VMC is not the direct course to the mark

Use your polar tables to determine the fastest route on a reach

Some polar tables have a pronounced bump that allows the extra speed gained by going faster and away from the mark to make up the extra distance sailed (VMG sailing works on exactly the same principle).

You would be right in asking the obvious question: if you start by sailing off at an angle to the course, how do you eventually get to the mark? The answer is that as you sail down the leg the VMC course and the course to the mark converge until they are the same.

You end up sailing a loop to the mark. Whether this loop is faster in total than just sailing the rhumb line would depend on the exact detail of the polar table.

Sailing to optimise VMC is really only going to work where the leg is a long one and you know the weather is going to change but have no idea how.

So let's imagine that you sail the optimum VMC and everybody else goes down the rhumb line. Halfway along the leg you are a couple of miles closer to the mark than everyone else when the wind drops out. There are a few hours of calm before the race starts again with a new wind direction. That couple of miles is then converted into a lead – so long as you are not disadvantaged by the new wind direction compared to the opposition.

But, given all that we have said about the approximate nature of polar tables, the wisdom of yachting off at a tangent to the rhumb line on a whim of the polar table does sound rather suspect ... and we would have to confess that we have only rarely done it.

This is a good moment to make a point about the use of polar tables in tactical situations.

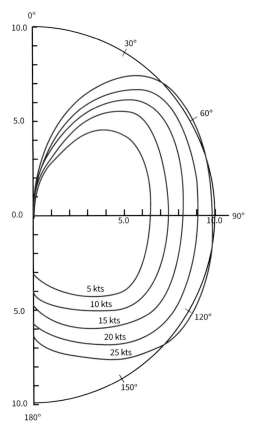

Because the shape of the polar table is similar for different wind speeds, wind gradient is not too great a problem for tactical applications of the polar table. We use the shape of the curve, rather than the precise numbers from it that are required by performance uses of the table

Despite all that we have said about the accuracy of polar tables, they do seem to work well in tactical applications. They are not too badly affected by the problems of wind sheer and gradient because they work from the shape of the polar curve more than the exact speed predicted.

Wind sheer means that the boat speed achieved at any particular wind angle and speed is inconsistent. But within a wind speed range of 4 or 5 knots the proportion of boat speed to angle represented by the shape of the curve is the same. Only extreme conditions of wind sheer will produce a sufficiently big gap between the measured wind speed at the masthead and the real wind force available, that it will make the polar table shape different. So tactical judgements from polar tables will work reasonably well, despite all the problems.

Going back to the reaching leg we had considered earlier, there are occasions where sailing off-course is highly recommended. This is when the leg is just a little bit too tight to hold a spinnaker all the way down it, so that if you do hoist you will end up low of the mark. The alternative is a two-sail reach all the way down the leg. It is a situation that you come across quite a lot and it is much quicker to put the spinnaker up and hold it as long as you can. You must judge the drop quite carefully so that you come in on a fast two-sail reach at the end.

We can see why the longer course works if we look at the polar table (opposite). There is usually a concavity between areas of the curve where the spinnaker is up and areas where you are two-sail reaching. This acts in the same way as the concavity in the polar between the different tacks going upwind, and the port and starboard gybe going downwind.

By sailing as high and as fast as you can with the spinnaker, and then dropping it and going as fast as you can with two sails up you are effectively 'tacking' down the reach – optimising your VMG just as you would upwind or downwind. It is a technique well established in the dinghy classes when you cannot lay a gybe mark with the spinnaker up. So you sail high and fast until the angle is such that you can hold the spinnaker and then hoist. Once it is up you can hold it round the mark and onto the next reach, following the same principle when dropping it to make the leeward mark.

Things get even more interesting when we apply the principles of VMC to the upwind and downwind legs.

Imagine the boat sailing towards the windward mark. The wind is blowing directly from the mark, and there is no current; then we can see that the optimum VMG course is the same as the optimum VMC course.

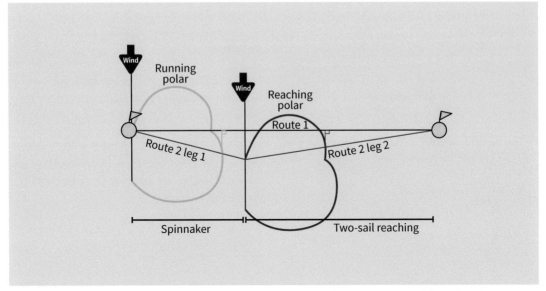

Using a spinnaker for part of a leg to optimise VMC – on route 2 you hit the maximum speeds from the polars

But if the wind shifts, we must rotate the polar table round to line up with the new wind direction. The optimum VMC and VMG courses no longer match – we can get to the windward mark faster by sailing at a different angle to the optimum VMG.

If we rotate the wind so that it has lifted us on this tack then we see that we should sail lower and faster to optimise our VMC to the mark.

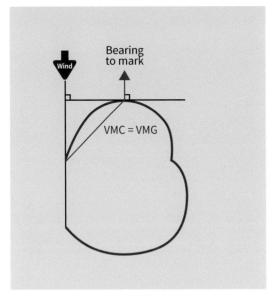

Sailing a VMC course upwind in windshifts: wind direction directly from the mark: VMC = VMG

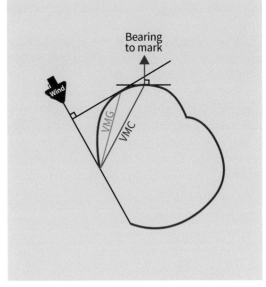

Sailing a VMC course upwind in windshifts: wind direction lifts compared to the mark bearing: boat speed for best VMC is lower and faster than VMG

If the wind heads us, then we should sail higher and slower.

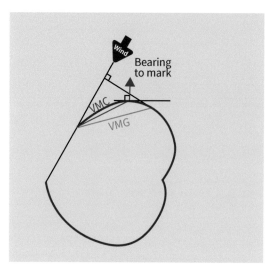

Sailing a VMC course upwind in wind shifts: wind direction heads compared to the mark bearing: boat speed for best VMC is higher and slower than VMG

If you are going to use this technique you will need a very accurate polar table, right down to the tenths of a knot that each couple of degrees of change in wind angle will give you – something that we have already written off as pretty much impossible.

However, that's not quite the case – and one place where the resources are available to make it possible is the America's Cup.

For the rest of us, without the resources of an America's Cup syndicate or such consistent wind conditions, developing the polar to that extent is still just about impossible. Nevertheless, the general rules can be applied: sail fast in the lifts and high in the headers. Not by much, perhaps just

a couple of tenths on the boat speed dial.

You will often find that this agrees with more general tactical rules. If you have got out to one side of the course and the fleet, when you get the header to tack back and consolidate you need to sail and cross as many boats as you can as fast as possible – so you sail fast on the lift that takes you across the fleet. Similarly, if you are trapped on a header by a boat to windward that will not tack, you can minimise your loses by holding high and slow and letting him sail over you quickly so that you can tack.

> **MARK:** It was the 1987 America's Cup in Fremantle, Perth where this technique was developed by the *Stars and Stripes* team. Not only did they have the time and resources to refine their polar tables to the necessary extent, but they were also blessed with remarkably consistent conditions of wind gradient and sheer.
>
> The Fremantle Doctor provided the perfect opportunity for this to work, allowing them to sail to a different target speed depending not only on the wind speed but also on the wind direction.
>
> So concerned were they that this should not fall into the hands of the other syndicates that there was considerable resistance to the placement of TV cameras on board *Stars and Stripes*. After finally agreeing they developed a code name for the information to hide its significance.

CHAPTER 6

Data Collection &

Performance Analysis

This is a topic that really needs its own book and a more qualified author, one with a PhD in statistics would just about get us there. Having made that disclaimer, we are going to restrict our comments to the practical experience we have had trying to optimise and record yacht performance.

Firstly, you should re-read the section on Polar Table Accuracy (page 26), where we discussed the limitations on the use of data collection and analysis to improve performance. The fundamental problem is that because you are only measuring wind speed in one place (at the masthead), you cannot know whether or not the wind gradient conditions are the same as the last time you collected data, even though the instruments might say they are.

One consequence of this is that the polar table itself is only an approximate record of the yacht's performance. It is possible for polar data collected one day to be half a knot out the next day – purely due to changes in wind gradient.

Overall, performance analysis has three main goals:

1. Checking and refining the calibration of the instrument system
2. The production of a general polar table that we can use – despite the problems with its accuracy – to sail the boat tactically as well as giving rough performance guides
3. Testing different configurations of the yacht: sails, mast set-ups, trimming and so on, and developing sail cross-over charts

SailingPerformance's Onboard Assistant allows you to tag the data

To achieve these goals the navigator or whoever is in charge has to be able to save sections of data and 'tag' them with short notes. That means adding some extra information to the datapoints – for example, which sail was being used. Both these tasks can usually be done using the main navigation software packages that are available. The computer can be set up to save the data automatically, and that should be covered by the manual so we will not focus on this. The most tricky and interesting part is tagging the data.

When we are sailing a lot of different things can happen that will impact performance. We might get covered by a competitor on a long leg, catch a plastic bag on the rudder, sail very close to shore with a strange wind gradient or have a technical issue on the sheeting point of the jib and have to sail very high and slow to fix it. None of these things will be automatically recorded, and they are very hard to remember when you come to analyse the data in the evening or, worse, a few days after the event. And yet, they will all have an impact on the data you record.

So it is very important that the navigator keeps notes about these events, with an indication of the time when they are happening. This will allow you to do the analysis and read the data in a much more effective and useful way.

To achieve this, it is important to establish a consistent system for tagging data, and make sure you stick to it during the season. Being consistent in the way you save and tag data is one of the keys to making the analysis easier and more useful.

Once you have saved and tagged your data, you can analyse it. So, how do we achieve our data analysis goals?

The first task is to look for periods of sailing at a reasonably consistent true wind angle and a reasonably consistent wind speed (each of these periods can be called tests or phases). How you find these periods depends on what set-up you have; some spreadsheets will graph the data and allow you to check it for consistency easily. Once you have found a likely looking set of data it is a matter of finding the average of the values involved: the true wind speed, angle and the boat speed.

If you wanted to be thorough you might set parameters for the figures, such as a minimum time limit on the set of data and a minimum standard deviation. In this way you can build up a collection of 'polar' points – data points that can fill a polar table – adding each one to the table as you go along.

Once you have these tests or 'phases' saved, you can use them for the real analysis.

Calibration

Looking at the data of the day can help in checking the calibration in many ways, with very specific checks or very general ones.

We have already mentioned that calculating the current is a complex process involving many different variables. So it gives a good indication when something is wrong. One of the first checks to do in your data is to see if the current direction and speed has been consistent (assuming we are not in tidal water!). Even in tidal water, we can check to see if the current is significantly different when we are on one tack or the other – this will quickly show up asymmetries in the calibrations.

But, if you have the time, you should check all the individual calibrations before you do any other analysis of the data, this includes checking:

- The boat speed calibration by checking the boat speed against the speed over ground in different tests
- The true wind speed as you go around the top mark: if it changes as you turn downwind there's probably an error (see diagram)
- The heading against the course over the ground during the day: there should be a difference between the two values, either because of leeway, current or both – but if you notice big differences from one tack to the other, or the differences don't align with what you know about the current or tide across the racecourse, then this points to an error in the compass calibration
- The true wind direction from tack to tack and gybe to gybe to make sure your wind calibration was correct
- All the other sensors for symmetry (for example, heel sensor, rudder sensor, etc.)

Wind sheer and gradient may affect the way the boat has been sailed on one tack or the other, but a consistent asymmetry during the day can either be a problem of calibration, or a problem of rig / keel asymmetry, which is even worse. In the latter case, you must check across several days of data to see if the asymmetry remains the same.

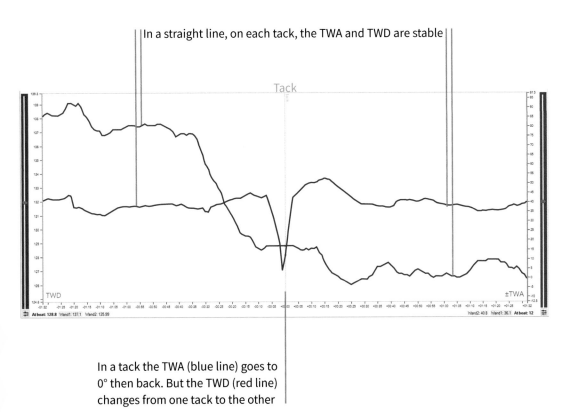

In a straight line, on each tack, the TWA and TWD are stable

Tack

TWD

±TWA

In a tack the TWA (blue line) goes to 0° then back. But the TWD (red line) changes from one tack to the other

The graph shows a tack and how this affects the TWD in a poorly calibrated boat.
The blue line shows the TWA and refers to the right vertical Y-Axis. The boat is initially going upwind at around 40° TWA. On the tack the TWA goes to 0° and then widens again.
The red line shows the TWD and refers to the left vertical Y-Axis. The TWD changes significantly during the tack, going from 138° to 128°.
On the same tack the TWD is quite constant (the red line is horizontal with small shifts), but as the boat tacks it changes rapidly.
This shows that the calibration is bad

There is a fundamental statistical concept at work here; the more data you collect, the more advantage you get from the 'law of large numbers'. A simple statement of this is that the more data you have, the better the results. In a single test / phase there is a good chance that something was anomalous: the calibration was wrong, the wind was doing something strange or the helmsman was thinking about his dinner plans rather than the telltales and trim. However, if you collect a lot of data, the averages get closer to the reality (especially if you take out the extreme values, called outliers). This is important for calibration, but also to achieve other data analytics goals.

Polar Tables

To create polar tables from scratch is really hard work. The job gets a lot easier if you have some figures to start with. However rough an approximation they are, it will at least give you a whole set of data that you can refine as you go along, rather than starting with a blank sheet of paper. This is where a VPP (see page 29) can be particularly useful as a start point.

The thing about polar tables is not to get too concerned about accuracy, there are such big problems with them that anything close to the rough shape will do a decent job for you. Plus or minus five percent, which would be a respectable error, gives you a one knot error range at ten knots boat speed. So don't get too psyched up about pinning down those hundredths of a knot that are sometimes on the display.

Once you have managed you and your team's expectations, you can get started on the work. Eventually there will be a lot of data points (usually drawn as dots in a polar diagram – see diagram below), each of which represents a set of 'test' data that you have collected.

Using these, you can adjust the polar table to more closely match the performance actually being achieved on the water. If you only have a small number of datapoints for a particular true wind speed and angle, it is important to be cautious when considering changing the polars because of them.

This whole procedure can be used for data collected during a day of racing, but also during a day of testing.

Let's say you want to refine you polars for the upwind targets in specific conditions. If the team has got time, the best way to do this is by setting up a test.

Get the helmsman to sail at a specific angle for short periods within the longer test. So, if it is an upwind test then they might start a fifteen-minute test by sailing at a target angle of 42° for five minutes. The rule is that they try to get the very best out of the boat, but they must stick as close as possible to that angle.

At the end of the five minutes the target angle is changed slightly, perhaps to 40°, and then again to 38° for the final five minutes.

This approach allows you to collect very specific and clean data, and that helps to get better target speeds for you to use.

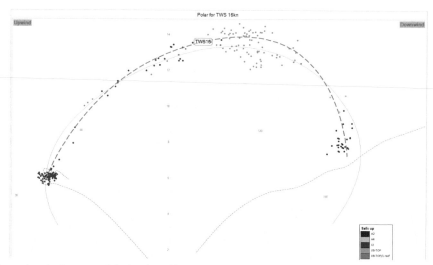

The line shows theorical targets while the dotted line shows targets built with tests on the water. Each test is a dot. The colour of the dot represents the sail used during the test. Chart from SailingPerformance

Configuration Testing

The last goal we can achieve with the analysis is to help with comparisons of the boat's configuration.

The knowledge of which configuration is better in a specific condition of wind and sea state is vital to winning regattas:

- Is the J1-A better or worse than the J1-B in 9kts?
- Does the rig setup with 10 shims perform better or worse than with 8 shims in 10kts?

All these questions are questions that we can group under the name of A / B testing or configuration testing.

The problem with testing in sailing is that it is hard to find conditions where wind gradient is the same, and this affects configuration testing. Let's say that on one day you go out and try a configuration for ten minutes. You save the data and then forget about it. Then you go out again a month later, and the true wind speed being measured is the same as for the first test, so you

decide to try another configuration and save the data. Then you go home and compare the two configurations. This can be very wrong and misleading, as the gradient could have been completely different on the two days.

There are two ways to tackle the problem. The first is to test different configurations on the same day (and with sails and rig configurations this is usually possible). The second is to put your trust in the law of large numbers, but that means that you will have to sail a lot more than two single tests with the two configurations.

Both ways are viable and will work – which you choose really depends on the team you are sailing with and the opportunities that are provided in the sailing programme.

Graphing the results of the tests is the usual way to understand the performance of a specific configuration and to see if one is better than the other. The diagram below shows an example of the analysis of different jibs.

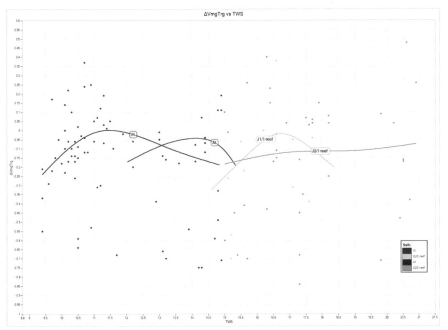

On the vertical (Y) axis is the delta VMG to the targets. The horizontal (X) axis is the wind speed. The coloured dots are tests and the lines show trends of each sail. Chart from SailingPerformance

Sail Charts

These types of analysis also come into play when you are building your sail chart. To find the crossover between one sail and the other you must repeat the process described above over and over again, sailing with the two sails in similar conditions and comparing the numbers.

Given the number of possible sail crossovers, this is quite a major task. Analysing data is a long and difficult job, but it is fundamental to having better numbers in the system and to sailing faster.

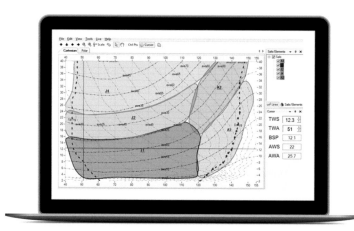

Sail crossover chart in SailingPerformance software

Ballast & Stacking Charts

The same approach can be used for ballast and stacking charts.

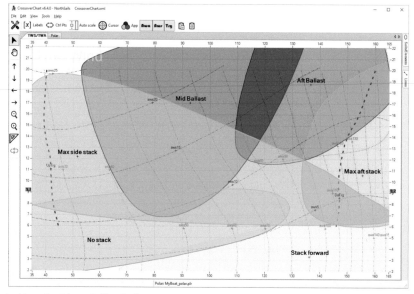

Ballast and stacking chart from SailingPerformance

Working As A Team

We want to finish this chapter by discussing something that is very important even if it is not strictly related to 'mastering the data'.

Data analysis in a team is not just a matter of sitting in front of a computer and using mathematical magic. When you talk about performance and configuration you are actually finding insights and discussing things that will be key to the trimmers, the tactician and other crew members.

It is fundamental that the group of people involved find a good way of sharing this information, discussing the results and findings and, overall, understanding each other's jobs and trusting each other. Getting the team to understand the importance of data and the navigator's role is key to succeeding in the job. And data analysis can play a big part in this.

Most of this task is performed off the boat, and it can be a great time to sit down with the team and share what you are doing and seeing in the numbers, explaining to them the logic, and making them more aware of what is happening 'under the hood' of the system.

There are some teams who want all the trimmers to receive a daily table of performance numbers, other teams that don't want to see any numbers at all. Each group of sailors has their own background and approach to the data.

We highly recommend that you work to make people aware of what is happening with the instruments and the computers on board, and also raise a hand when you notice, for example, that the calibration was bad.

Sometimes saying "sorry guys, today we had an issue with the paddlewheel so speed numbers might have been off in the second leg" is a great way of making the team build trust in you. There's every chance that the trimmers and helmsmen noticed that the boat speed was really low in that last leg but didn't say anything. They don't know whether to attribute it to the instruments, the boat set-up or weed on the rudder – and if you can provide a solid explanation then that will give them faith that you know what you are doing.

Data analysis will provide better numbers on the water, help the team to take critical decisions on set-ups and configurations, and help you to get the team 'on the same page' with you and the system. It's not an easy job, but it's worth doing!

Don't just celebrate your performance, sit down afterwards and discuss the data output

CHAPTER 7

What's Next?

In this book we have seen many aspects of how an instrument system and the data it provides can be leveraged to optimise the performance of a team and a boat. We have explained the role of the navigator in the key moments of the regatta and the skills that he or she has to develop to do a great job.

Most importantly, as we have said at the beginning of the book, we have tried to do all of this while remaining as agnostic as possible from specific systems, so that the reader can develop a mindset and a knowledge that goes beyond the instructions for the use of one or other piece of navigation software or instrument system. We believe that this approach is invaluable and the most effective in providing a solid foundation in the topic.

However, we can't ignore that the technologies on board race boats are evolving at an ever-increasing speed. It's likely that there will soon be new methods and ways to do things that might become mainstream, ones that we have not touched on in this book.

This is the era of big data, artificial intelligence (AI) and machine learning. There are researchers and businesses outside the marine industry that are training computers to assist with decisions in areas as diverse as the criminal system and healthcare. Computers and machines are becoming steadily better at both creative and analytical jobs and, in some areas, they are as good or better than a human.

How long until these aspects of the technology hit the sailing world?

We have America's Cup teams issuing press releases about employing AI experts to try to approach their data analysis in a new way.

We already have an America's Cup class rule for the AC75 that goes to great lengths to stop autopilots from driving the boats – because they are so effective.

Outside the America's Cup, others are already training advanced algorithms to provide better autopilot systems for short-handed offshore racing. Mark was involved with a (non-America's Cup) sail shape measurement system that employed machine learning routines, and the same techniques are being used in object detection to prevent crashes at sea.

More and more of these technologies are coming into our world. The role of the navigator will be to understand how they work, understand their potential and their limits, and integrate them into the workflow.

Soon navigation software might suggest true wind angle calibrations, and auto-fill the 'What If' scenario by automatically looking at the position relative to the rest of the fleet and the wind, suggesting a lee bow to the tactician before he even asks.

The navigator's role will evolve again, but most of the things written in this book will still be valid, and understanding the logic behind all of this will still make you a better sailor and a better navigator.

We hope you enjoyed the book and can bring the ideas to focus on your own sailing.

CREDITS

The authors and publisher would likely to thank the numerous groups and individuals who have made this book possible.

OUR SPONSORS whose enthusiasm for and contribution to the project has been fantastic:
A+T Instruments
Expedition navigation and sailing software
SailingPerformance

IAN WALKER for his brilliant Foreword

OUR PHOTOGRAPHERS / IMAGE CREATORS who own the copyrights for their images:
ClubSwan Racing | Studio Borlenghi: Pages 6, 15 (bottom), 16, 20, 25, 29, 30, 33, 55, 63, 72, 73, 77, 79, 89, 90
The Stella Maris team | Antonio Otero: Front cover, Back cover, Pages 5 (bottom), 12
A+T Instruments: Pages 18, 19, 41, 42, 47
Expedition: Pages 21, 22, 24, 70, 71, 77
SailingPerformance: Pages 26, 28, 31, 83, 85, 86, 87, 88
Mike Mottl: Back cover, Page 5 (top)
North Sails: Page 8
Sedat Yilmaz: Page 13
Timaldo / Shutterstock: Page 15 (top)
BT1976 / Shutterstock: Page 34
Mike1024 / Wikipedia: Page 40
Jeremy Atkins: Page 46
gaynor5 / Pixabay: Page 60
Alvov / Shutterstock: Page 68

SAIL TRIMMING

Here are some great books to take your racing to the next level

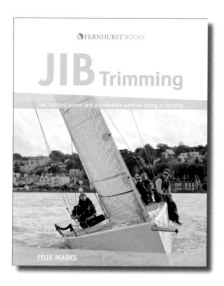

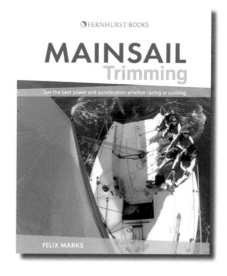

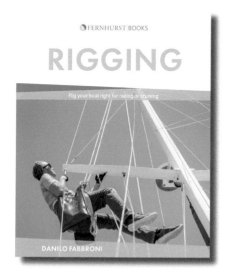

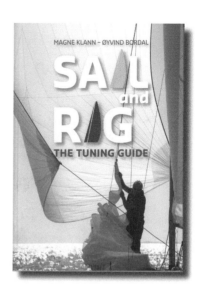

RACING RULES

When the windward mark is an obstruction

> Could I hail for room to tack?

This situation occurs only when the mark is also an obstruction (other than a starting mark when approaching the line to start). The mark might be a large metal buoy or a boat (maybe displaying flag M, replacing the original mark that has drifted out of place).

You are A.
• Provided that you need to tack, and you are certain the other boat is not fetching the mark, you may hail to B for room to tack. 'Water' may be misunderstood; 'Room to tack' is best. **(Rule 20.1)**
• If B hails 'You tack' in response to your hail, and then ducks your stern or crosses safely ahead of you and fetches the mark, you have broken a rule (because you had no right to hail). If he is aggrieved you must take a penalty, or he could protest you. If he responds to your hail by tacking, he might protest and claim in a protest hearing that he could have layed the mark, or that you could have easily sailed below the mark. **(Rule 20.1)**
• If you judge that B can get round the mark without passing head to wind, you are still the right-of-way boat provided you don't pass head to wind yourself. So even if you don't have luffing rights, you may go up to head to wind in order to 'shoot the mark', and B must keep clear. **(Rule 11 & Definition Proper Course)**
• For you to have the right to hail, you have to be close-hauled or above and on a course from which you must make a substantial change to avoid

the obstruction. If you were further to leeward, so that the obstruction was not in your path, then you would not have the right to hail; you would have to slow down and tack behind B or bear away and gybe. **(Definition Obstruction)**
• If you do hail for room to tack, you must tack as soon as there is room. You can't hail and then 'shoot the mark' by going head to wind and bearing away around the mark. **(Rule 20.2(d))**

You are B:
• As the windward boat you must keep clear if A luffs in an attempt to 'shoot the mark'. If he luffs as needed to shoot the mark he does not have to give you room to keep clear. **(Rules 11 & 43.1(b))**
• If A hails for room to tack, even if you are sure that you could get round the mark without tacking, you must respond to the hail (by tacking or hailing 'You tack'). You cannot just tell A that he has no right to hail for room to tack. **(Rule 20.2(b))**
• If A hails for room to tack, and you are not sure that you can get round the mark without tacking, then you must either tack or hail back 'You tack' and give room to A to tack. **(Rules 20.2(b) & (c))**

8

9. On the Reach

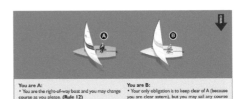

You are A:
• You are the right-of-way boat and you may change course as you please. **(Rule 12)**

You are B:
• Your only obligation is to keep clear of A (because you are clear astern), but you may sail any course you like. **(Rule 12)**

You are A:
• With B aiming to overtake you on your leeward side, you might be happy not to manoeuvre in case doing so discourages him, and he decides to take your wind on your windward side.
• On the other hand if you are approaching a port hand mark, you don't want him to get an inside overlap, so you may bear away to encourage him to stay to windward.
• While clear ahead, you remain the right-of-way boat and may luff or bear away as you please.

You are B:
• As you are clear astern you must keep clear, but you may luff or bear away as you please.

9

UNDERSTAND THE WIND

WIND STRATEGY

David Houghton & Fiona Campbell

SAIL TO WIN

"Wind Strategy remains the 'go-to' book for racing sailors seeking to improve their understanding of the vagaries of the wind."

Yachting Life

CHAPTER 5

Wind Facts: Gusts & Lulls

The wind varies on every timescale, from seconds to minutes to hours to days and even longer. It is the short period variations in the order of minutes which are normally described as gusts and lulls.

Gusts & Lulls Due To Thermal Overturning

We saw in Chapter 2 that many gusts and lulls are a result of air overturning near the sea or land surface when the air aloft, which has not been slowed or backed by friction at the surface, comes down to replace what has been subject to friction. A common cause of this overturning is thermal; when air warmed at the surface becomes buoyant, rises, and is replaced by air from aloft. This is the most easy to understand.

On many days, particularly when there is a regular pattern of cumulus clouds, the gusts and lulls arrive at fairly regular intervals. In these conditions the normal surface wind is blowing in the normal way and super-imposed on it is an overturning motion, upwards underneath the cumulus clouds and downwards between them (below). The descending air has not experienced friction near the surface so it has approximately the horizontal speed and direction of the gradient wind. It is significantly veered and stronger than the wind which has spent some time near the

surface. In other words it is a gust. The air under each cloud has spent time near the surface, has been slowed and backed by friction - it is a lull. Thermally driven gusts and lulls have one clearly defined characteristic: a gust is always veered and stronger in contrast with a lull, which is always backed and lighter.

Timescale & Size Of Shift

If the cumulus clouds are small and relatively close together they indicate a relatively short time between gusts and lulls - perhaps 3 minutes or so. The swing in wind is typically in the order of 5 to 10 degrees in direction and 5 to 10 per cent in speed. If the clouds are larger and further apart a longer time interval is indicated - perhaps 10 to 15 minutes - and the shifts may be less regular and larger. If the convection becomes so deep that the cumulus clouds turn into cumulonimbus and showers develop, completely different wind characteristics are experienced. They are described in Chapter 15.

Gusts & Lulls Due To Mechanical Mixing

'Mechanical mixing' simply describes what happens with air moving over the earth's surface when the air is far from homogeneous and the surface is far from smooth. There is a continuous stream of fluctuations in the wind, both in speed and direction. Recordings of these fluctuations show an equal and random incidence of increases and decreases, veers and backs, with no discernable pattern of veering in gusts or backing in lulls.

Gusts & Lulls Inshore With An Offshore Wind

If the wind is blowing across the coast from land to sea you would expect that every gust would be stronger and more veered because of the lower friction over the water. And this is what sailors experience, gust and veer / lull and back going together, at least until the adaptation is complete, which may be any distance from 1 to 5 kilometres downwind from the coast, depending on the stability of the air (as in Chapter 2).

Gusts & Lulls At Sea & Near The Coast With An Onshore Wind

Over the sea where the surface temperature is relatively uniform you will usually find fairly regular patterns in the wind which can be timed and anticipated.

The most regular of all are in the trade winds, where row upon row of small cumulus clouds extend for hundreds of miles, each individual

Rows of small cumulus clouds

cloud indicating air rising beneath the cloud to be replaced by air moving downwards in the adjacent clear space between the clouds (see p67).

Near the coast an onshore wind brings with it all the characteristics of the open ocean.

Absence of cumulus clouds does not mean that there is no sequence of gusts and lulls. It could merely be that the air is too dry for clouds to form.

Gusts & Lulls Inland

Over land the pattern of gusts and lulls is usually very irregular. For one thing, the rise in temperature of the land surface depends on both its dryness and its colour, both of which vary greatly from place to place. Black tarmac for instance can easily be more than 10°C warmer than an adjacent grass area. Sailors on small inland lakes have to take the gusts and lulls as they come, but timing the gust / lull sequence before the start of every race is still a useful practice. Some element of short period coherence is often experienced.

Does The Wind Always Veer In A Gust?

The straight answer is 'No!' Gust and veer is the pattern typically associated with cumulus clouds in the Northern Hemisphere, and you can bank on it in moderate to fresh winds when the air is unstable to the sea temperature, and also near the coast with an offshore wind. But in stable air and when the wind is strong, and also over land, do not expect any preference. And if you are beating in towards the land within 5 km downwind from the coast expect the wind to back as you close the shore. An out-of-sequence backing or veering gust over the open sea may be the first indication of a new wind approaching.

Tactics

Always time the gust / lull sequence before the start of every race and note any bias towards a particular pattern.

Squalls, Billows & Surface Gravity Currents

These could all be called gusts, but they are discussed individually elsewhere (see Chapters 13 & 14).

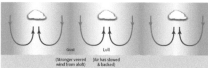

Gust   Lull

(Stronger veered wind from aloft)   (Air has slowed & backed)

The clouds causing gusts & lulls

28

29

FERNHURST
BOOKS

We hope you enjoyed this book

If you did, **please post a review on Amazon**

Discover more books on

SAILING · RACING · CRUISING · MOTOR BOATING

SWIMMING · DIVING · SURFING

PADDLING · FISHING

View our full range of titles at **www.fernhurstbooks.com**

Sign up to receive details of new books & exclusive special offers at

www.fernhurstbooks.com/register

Get to know us more on **social media**